REVELATIONS 2024 – TO THE PEOPLE OF THE U.S. HOUSE OF JUSTICE:

A SUMMONS TO END THE "TRUMP SHOW" BEFORE IT ENDS THE UNITED STATES

KARL KRAUS

ALSO BY KARL KRAUS:

What Does Resistance Mean Now?:
A Political Strategy to Crush Trumpfascism
(2021)

For all true resisters – between past and future

Editor's Note:

As this book was being prepared for press, on February 28, 2024, the Supreme Court of the United States made a fateful decision to stay the prosecution of Donald Trump *until at least the end of April,* to allow the Court to "reconsider" a patently absurd and unconstitutional argument claiming that a president should be granted "full immunity" from prosecution for any violations of law.

The U.S. Supreme Court has thereby granted undue respect to an argument that would place all presidents above the law, and effectively render the basic founding principle of our constitution and system of justice null and void. On top of this, the Justices of our Supreme Court have made a decision that may keep the people of the United States from ever seeing a trial of Trump for his participation in the Insurrection of January 6, 2021 that disgraced our Capitol and for the first time ever in U.S. history broke our long tradition of peaceful transfers of presidential power.

Since the events of justice in 2024 will determine whether our constitutional system of government survives into the years ahead, let us hope the Justices of our Supreme Court, along with all Americans, pay heed to the words of this book, and its summons to accountability:

"And fearless are they who not only read
but hear and act on these words:
for the time is at hand."

CONTENTS

A Summons to the U.S. "House of Justice"

Introduction:
A Summons, a Call, and a Warning from History –
"Where law ends, tyranny begins."

I.
Indictments Rendered
against the
U.S. House of Justice (All of Us)

II.
Argument:
The "Facts of the Case"

III.
Judgments Issued
to the U.S. House of Justice

Epilogue
A Call to Action: ENOUGH!

*Forthcoming (May 2024):
A Political Strategy for
Crushing the Fascist Beast of Trumpism*

A refusal to know is already part of the disaster.

—Karl Jaspers, *The Future of Mankind, 1961*

All I have is a voice
To undo the folded lie,
The romantic lie in the brain
Of the sensual man-in-the-street
And the lie of Authority
Whose buildings grope the sky

—W.H. Auden, *"September 1, 1939"*

A Summons to the U.S. "House of Justice"* in 2024

(A *Preface* to *Undoing the Folded Lie of Trumpism,* forthcoming in 2024, by Karl Kraus)

**Note:*
The U.S. House of Justice
= All of Us!

Introduction:

A Summons, a Call, &
A Warning from History –

"Where Law Ends, Tyranny Begins"

The glory of the Infinite is the egress of the subject from the dark corners of its reserve, which might offer an escape route from the **summons of the other**... *Glory is the response to the summons* without any possible evasion. (Emmanuel Levinas, "Truth of Disclosure and Truth of Testimony," 1972)

We think in community **with others**. (Immanuel Kant, *Critique of Pure Reason*)

A Summons, A Call, &
A Warning from History –

"Where Law Ends, Tyranny Begins":

A *Call to Action* against Fascism in our Times

A refusal to know is already part of the disaster.
(Karl Jaspers, *The Future of Mankind,* 1961)

Historical *processes* are created and constantly *interrupted* by human initiative, by the *initium* man is insofar as he is an acting being. Hence it is not in the least superstitious, it is even a counsel of realism, to look for the unforeseeable and unpredictable, to be prepared for and to expect 'miracles' in the political realm. And the more heavily the scales are weighted in favor of disaster, the more miraculous will the deed done in freedom appear; *for it is disaster, not salvation, which always happens automatically and therefore always must appear to be irresistible.* Objectively, that is, seen from the outside and without taking into account that man is a beginning and a beginner, the chances that tomorrow will be like yesterday are always overwhelming. (Hannah Arendt, "What is Freedom?" *Between Past and Future,* 1961)

The Warning

In 1947 a former inmate of Buchenwald gave testimony to his understanding of the political meaning of the systematic staging of the NAZI's terrorizing cult of power:

> The triumph of [of totalitarian fascism] demands that the tortured victim allow himself to be led to the noose without protesting, that he renounce and abandon himself to the point of ceasing to affirm his identity. And [this] is not for nothing... They know that the system which succeeds in destroying its victim before he mounts the scaffold...is incomparably the best for keeping a whole people in slavery. In submission. Nothing is more terrible than these processions of human beings going like dummies to their deaths. (David Rousset, Buchenwald inmate, *Les Jours de notre mort,* 1947)

In light of this testimony from the pit of totalitarian power in the twentieth century, a core set of existential political questions now face ALL Americans, and especially the Justices of the U.S. Supreme Court:

Through our lack of decisive political action to ban four-times criminally-indicted Trump from being able to run for the highest office of the land by implementing the force of law at our disposal via the "clear command" given to us by the disqualification clause of the 14th Amendment of our Constitution – as Judge Michael Luttig has so eloquently explicated – we are running the risk of renouncing and abandoning ourselves to the point of ceasing to affirm both our individual and national identities as citizens of a democratic republic.

In the face of this supreme existential risk, we must now ask ourselves: Are we all, through our failures of political vision and action, thereby effectively colluding with the Trump Show to destroy our democratic identities and political constitution even before we mount the scaffold of our 2024 elections? And are we thereby abjectly submitting ourselves to political slavery even before the November elections occur?

As the future looks back on the apocalyptic year of 2024, will we – by our continuing failure to act – allow it to render this judgment on all of us (as we render judgment on the Germans who failed to unite to act decisively in the years leading up to 1933): "Nothing was more terrible than watching the procession of Americans going like dummies to their constitutional death"?

These are the haunting questions that animate and echo through the words of this indictment and summons to action –

All over the world I dread the self-deception which we have experienced – that this could not happen here. It can happen anywhere. It is improbable only where the broad masses of the population are aware of the possible menace and thus will not be lulled into security; where they know the type of totalitarianism and will recognize it in its rudimentary stages and in each of its manifestations – this Proteus who keeps appearing in ever new masks, *who slips eel-like out of our grasp, who does the opposite of what he says, who distorts the meaning of words, who speaks not in order to communicate or tell the truth, but in order to numb, to distract, to hypnotize, to intimidate, to dupe – who will exploit and evoke every fear, and will promise security and utterly wreck it at the same time.* (Karl Jaspers, "The Fight Against Totalitarianism," *Philosophy and the World*, 1963)

If we want to fight fascism, we must understand it. **Wishful thinking will not help us.** (Erich Fromm, *Escape from Freedom*, 1941)

The Summons to the U.S. House of Justice (in the words for opening a session before the Justices of the *U.S. Supreme Court*):

"Oyez, Oyez, Oyez (Hear Ye, Hear Ye, Hear Ye): All persons having business before the Honorable, the Supreme Court of the United States, are admonished to draw near and give their attention."

And in the words of another ancient call to attention, appropriate to our own apocalyptic moment in history as a summons to all people within the U.S. House of Justice to "Come" and pay attention to the words being offered here as a warning and guide for action:

> I hear behind me a great voice, like that of a shofar. It says: What you see, write it and send it to the communities...
>
> The Spirit and the promised say, Come. Let the hearer respond: Come. Let the thirsty come. And whosoever will, let them take the water of life freely. I myself testify to every hearer of the words of this inspiration...
>
> And fearless are they who not only read but hear and act on these words: for the time is at hand. (*The Book of Revelation* 22:17-18; 1:3, 10-11)
>
> The glory of the Infinite is the egress of the subject from the dark corners of its reserve, which might offer an escape route from the summons of the other... Glory is the response to the summons without any possible evasion. (Levinas, "Truth of Disclosure and Truth of Testimony," 1972)

The Trump Show's Campaign for Permission to Install a Totalitarian Dictatorship

> The longer one listened to him, the more obvious it became that his inability to speak was closely connected with *an inability to think*, namely, *to think from the standpoint of somebody else*... Nothing could have demonstrated this more convincingly than the grotesque silliness of his last words... It

A totally corrupt man, enabled by a sycophantic and cowardly political party to campaign again for president of the United States in 2024, has made vividly clear his full intent to overthrow the structures of the U.S. Constitution if he wins the November election. In the opening days of 2024 this man, who personifies what Hannah Arendt meant by the *banality of evil* – the mindless inability to think with regard for others – appealed to the U.S. House of Justice (in which all people of the U.S. are responsible decision-makers) to grant him a permission structure for nothing less than the creation of a totalitarian dictatorship.

Trump's demand for such permission was issued (IN ALL CAPS) through his January 18th 2024 "Truth Social" appeal to the Supreme Court for absolute immunity, to ensure that this next time as president he will have the absolute power of a dictator to do anything he wants to "cross the line," with no accountability to the structures of U.S. constitutional law or justice:

"A PRESIDENT OF THE UNITED STATES MUST
HAVE FULL IMMUNITY, WITHOUT WHICH IT
WOULD BE IMPOSSIBLE FOR HIM/HER TO
PROPERLY FUNCTION…

"EVEN EVENTS THAT 'CROSS THE LINE' MUST
FALL UNDER TOTAL IMMUNITY, OR IT WILL BE
YEARS OF TRAUMA TRYING TO DETERMINE GOOD
FROM BAD… [And "crossing the line," according to
Trump's lawyers, could include the political
assassination of rivals for political office!]

"ALL PRESIDENTS MUST HAVE COMPLETE &
TOTAL PRESIDENTIAL IMMUNITY, OR THE
AUTHORITY & DECISIVENESS OF A PRESIDENT OF
THE UNITED STATES WILL BE STRIPPED & GONE
FOREVER.

"**HOPEFULLY THIS WILL BE AN EASY DECISION.
GOD BLESS THE SUPREME COURT!**" (D. Trump,
2024)

*****

To the Supreme Court:

Responsibility for the other precedes every
decision, it is before the origin… **[R]esponsibility
moves positively toward the other.** (Emmanuel
Levinas, "Truth of Disclosure and Truth of
Testimony," 1972)

With fundamental responsibility for justice in mind,

deciding whether Trump should be granted, unlike any

other president before him, "absolute immunity" from

prosecution should indeed be a swift and "easy decision"

for the U.S. Supreme Court – as the U.S. Circuit Court of Appeals in D.C. made clear in its recent unanimous decision of February 6, 2024 – if indeed it even accepts such a craven appeal/demand for criminal absolution beyond the decision of the Circuit Court.

Section 3 of Article One of the Constitution clearly states that anyone impeached by Congress is still also "subject to Indictment, Trial, Judgment and Punishment, according to Law," underlining one of our fundamental constitutional principles, which is that NO ONE, including the President of the United States, is above the law. Therefore by insisting on absolute presidential immunity from prosecution in an appeal directly to the Supreme Court, Trump is again not only illustrating his full intent to overthrow the fundamental rules and structure of our Constitution and its structure of limited power for presidents – balanced against and not superior to, the powers of Congress and the Supreme Court – but is asking the Court to grant him permission to assume the powers of a totalitarian dictator who would be completely above the law if he were to regain the powers of the Presidency.

As legal scholars have noted, not only is such a claim absurd in the face of U.S. constitutional law, but it is also absurd in the face of our history, since all 44 presidents before Trump were able to "function" as Presidents without the kind of absolute immunity that Trump is seeking to be granted in defiance of all logic and U.S. constitutional principle. Prior to the questionable and arguably unconstitutional grant of limited presidential immunity from prosecution while in office created by the Justice Department's administrative "memo" in response to Nixon's Watergate crimes (a grant of immunity which should be revoked by Congress as soon as possible!), previous presidents were fully liable to criminal arrest while in office even for such simple things as speeding in the streets. As far as "original intent" goes, when president Ulysses Grant was caught speeding in a carriage through the streets of Washington in the nineteenth century, he was arrested and had to pay a fine immediately.

And even after the Justice Department's limited grant of immunity to prosecution while in office, presidents have remained fully liable to prosecution after serving in office, as president Clinton admitted in his plea deal to avoid prosecution after he left office, and as Mitch McConnell himself clearly stated would be the case for Trump after January 20, 2021. This, in fact, was one of the reasons Trump tried so desperately to remain in office – so he would not have to face the inevitable criminal prosecutions to come.

But Trump and his sycophantic enablers are now seeking from our U.S. House of Justice – through the guise of the Trump Show's 2024 presidential campaign – the *permission structure* to overthrow our Constitution and install a totalitarian dictatorship in 2025. So the existential question facing all of us who live within, and are responsible for, the U.S. House of Justice in 2024 is:

*Will we hand Trump what he wants, as the Germans did for Hitler in January 1933, or **will we act decisively in 2024 to shut the Trump Show down** and commit it to the bin of historical horrors where it belongs?*

A Warning from 100 Years Ago re: Hitler's Trial for his 1923 Failed Insurrection

Unlike the long delays for the trials of D.J. Trump, even after the four criminal indictments of 2023, the high treason trial of Adolf Hitler and his fellow insurrectionists for the failed November 1923 Munich "Beer Hall Putsch," which was directed at the overthrow of the German democratic constitution, began *within four months* of Hitler's failed insurrection, **on Feb. 26, 1924**. "High Treason" was defined in the German law code as the attempt to change the constitution of Germany by violent means.

As "we the people" of the U.S. House of Justice continue to be forced to wait – more than three years after the January 2021 insurrection and more than eight months after the four criminal indictments (and 92 criminal charges) were issued in 2023 – to see justice done through the criminal trials of Trump, we should pause to consider, as both omen and historical warning, the haunting coincidence of the fact that the first criminal trial of Trump is set to begin in March 2024 in such close proximity to the 100th anniversary of the farcically botched March 1924 criminal trial of Adolf Hitler.

The tragic world-historic farce of the 1924 "trial" was that it allowed Hitler to use the Munich courtroom as a national platform not only for broadcasting Nazi propaganda, but to launch his political campaign to consolidate the base of power he would need to complete the overthrow of the German democratic constitution that he and his Nazi followers first attempted in 1923. Within months of being handed the reins of political power in January 1933, Hitler succeeded in overthrowing the federal constitution he had been allowed to attack throughout the 1924 trial, transforming the trial into the launch of his national campaign for the destruction of German democracy. This happened because the public narrative of Hitler's trial was allowed to be dictated by the rhetoric of Hitler and his fellow insurrectionists, effectively nullifying the attempts of the Judge, prosecutor, and government to ensure that justice was seen to be done to protect the German constitution.

As historian David King concludes: "It was there in the [1924] Munich courtroom that Adolf Hitler could have been eliminated from the scene and perhaps forgotten. Instead, this haunting perversion of justice paved the way for the Third Reich and allowed Adolf Hitler to unleash the most unimaginable suffering upon humanity" (David King, *The Trial of Adolf Hitler*, 2017).

With this historical warning about the way failed trials of fascist tyrants can have potentially apocalyptic results for constitutional democracy, all citizens of the United States must recognize that 2024 will compel existential judgments of the highest historical import from our U.S. "House of Justice" both within and outside of the courtrooms hosting Trump's criminal trials. And these judgments will not only be the verdicts rendered by our courts of law, but judgments rendered by every American as each of us decides our course of political action to determine the outcome of this potentially apocalyptic year for the United States and our constitutional democracy.

Hitler was handed the reins of German political power in January 1933, and within a year had transformed Germany into a totalitarian dictatorship. Will we Americans make the same mistake in 2024 by allowing our election to turn the reins of power over to a man who has declared, just as Hitler did in *Mein Kampf* long before he was handed the reins of power in 1933, his commitment to the overthrow of the existing Constitution?

*****

> The triumph of [of totalitarian fascism] demands that the tortured victim allow himself to be led to the noose without protesting, that he renounce and abandon himself to the point of ceasing to affirm his identity. And [this] is not for nothing... They know that the system which succeeds in destroying its victim before he mounts the scaffold...is incomparably the best for keeping a whole people in slavery. In submission. Nothing is more terrible than these processions of human beings going like dummies to their deaths. (David Rousset, Buchenwald inmate, *Les Jours de notre mort*, 1947)

David Rousset's testimony, spoken out of the Holocaust's heart of darkness, addressed the political theatrics of an entire people's willing renunciation of identity, which began with the willing handover of the reins of German government to Hitler and his Nazi movement in January of 1933, a handover of political power that quickly opened the way to a nation's terrorized submission to political slavery, which culminated in World War and the Holocaust. In light of this striking testimony, ALL Americans should be asking the most basic existential political questions as we struggle to come to judgments about what we each will DO in the historically pivotal year of 2024, during which all Americans will determine – through our action or inaction (as dictated by our failures of imagination) – whether Trump and his fascist movement are allowed to take control of the government of the United States in 2025.

The most fundamental question of all is this: Are we, by our failures of thinking and our inaction in the face of the ongoing Trump Campaign Show and its manipulation of all the institutional levers of our ethically and politically compromised media, repeating the mistakes of the past - not only of our own past in 2016, but that of the Germans from 1924 to 1933, by ALLOWING ourselves to be mindlessly led to the noose of our constitutional demise without any serious thinking and action to interdict the projected end of our Republic by a band of fascist coup plotters and their Fuhrer?

Are we – by our lack of imaginative political action to ban four-times criminally-indicted Trump from being able to run for the highest office of the land – renouncing and abandoning ourselves to the point of ceasing to affirm both our individual and national identities as citizens of a democratic Republic? And are we all, by our lack of imagination and action, thereby effectively colluding with the Trump Show in destroying our democratic identities along with our Constitution long before we mount the scaffold of our 2024 elections? Will we, by our failures to act in 2024, allow history to say of all of us, as it looks back on the apocalyptic year of 2024, "Nothing was more terrible than watching the procession of Americans going like dummies to their constitutional death"?

> Tyranny is the cooperation of parasite and host; no tyrant maintains himself by force [alone], but by trading on his victims' fears... Tyranny is seldom (in the long run, never) imposed on people from without; it is a projection of their own pusillanimity... Hence the duty of the imaginative is to force this issue and compel decisions. (Northrop Frye, *Fearful Symmetry*, 1947)

In the ebbing days of 2023, even as the New York civil fraud trial of the Trump business highlighted and foreshadowed the coming melodramatics of the 2024 Trump Show, we witnessed on a daily basis the incomprehensibly weak and continually waffling attempts of our court system to impose even limited gag orders on Trump to prevent the most egregious of his terrorizing attacks on judges, prosecutors and potential witnesses. Thus we have witnessed the process by which

ALL Americans have already become the "tortured victims" of the Trump Show that, even in the face of the four different criminal indictments of 2023, has been allowed to continue its fascist planning, funding, propagandizing, and coordinating of the organized political power needed to destroy our Republic.

And so the people of the United States are already becoming "tortured victims" of a developing movement of totalitarian fascism, which most of the leadership of our country in both government and the media has barely begun to seriously analyze. Indeed, many of our leaders in politics and the media can't even seem to bring themselves to explicitly use the word "fascist" (rather than the often-used vague terms "authoritarian" or "autocratic") to accurately and precisely label what the Trumpist movement and its G.O.P. vehicle of sycophantic support have become. And lacking the vision to precisely label the form of political power and the specific threat we are facing, neither we nor our leaders can begin to think about their responsibilities for action to resist the ongoing campaign to make us all victims of a fascist overthrow of our institutional powers of self-government. And in the absence of such clear thinking, we have proven ourselves incapable of organizing an effective political counterforce capable of attacking and dismantling this fascist movement in the ways demanded by such a direct threat to our constitutional democracy.

This willed unconsciousness of non-thinking, this sleepwalking inaction of ourselves and our national leadership through the history of the last eight years (2015-2023) is exactly what the "triumph" of totalitarian fascism "demands" of its "tortured victims." For it is precisely our twinned failures to think imaginatively and to act, our failures to even admit we are dealing with an organized totalitarian fascist movement to overthrow our democracy, that will constitute the primary evidence for future historians who will have to explain how an entire nation of Americans, who viewed themselves as proud members of a democracy, allowed themselves "to be led to the noose without protesting," and thereby "renounce[ed] and abandon[ed] [themselves] to the point of ceasing to affirm [their] identity."

And IF we Americans allow this to be our historical fate in 2024, then we will have no one to blame but ourselves, since we have not only the clear historical warning of the millions of victims slaughtered during the totalitarian holocausts of the twentieth century, but also the words and vivid testimonies of all those who survived the Holocaust's "Pit of Destruction," to warn and remind us that IF we continue to sleepwalk politically through the year 2024 and fail to act, we will be granting the MAGA fascist movement exactly what it most needs to achieve its political and historical goals.

For "it is not for nothing" that the Trump Show wants us to simply accede the historical development of 2024 to the manipulative power of its constant barrage of propaganda, so it can distract us from thinking and acting on the lessons of the past. The entire objective of the Trump Show is to distract us from decisive action against it so we ALLOW ourselves "to be led to the noose without protesting," and thereby "renounce and abandon [ourselves] to the point of ceasing to affirm [our] identity" as free citizens of a democratic Republic.

The producers of the Trump Show have learned well not only from Nazi history but from their chief contemporary mentor in Russia that "the system which succeeds in destroying its victim before he mounts the scaffold... is incomparably the best" not only for keeping but for leading a whole people - an entire nation - into slavish submission. **So if we, as Americans, do not want to concede the history of 2024 and beyond to the totalitarian producers of the Trump Show, it is time for us all to wake up and organize ourselves to ACT to ensure the Trump Show is deprived of the means (both financial and communicative) to play itself out on our national stage during the remainder of 2024.**

It is way past time for the citizens and institutions of American democracy to rise to action to *shut down the Trump Show* in order to preserve our own freedom as well as our individual identities and the identity of our Nation as a constitutional Republic governed by the "rule of law" rather than the arbitrary rule of tyrannical men. For, indeed, "Nothing is more terrible than these processions of human beings going like dummies to their deaths." And if we fail to Act to dismantle the power of the Trump Show to continue to direct our national drama in 2024, we will betray our most fundamental existential duty as both human beings and citizens of a democracy. For in 2024 our most fundamental duty as citizens "to preserve, protect and defend the Constitution" is to ensure that we DO NOT ALLOW ourselves and each other to play submissive roles as part of a zombified "procession of Americans marching like dummies to our constitutional death."

*****

> The serious threat to our democracy is not the existence of foreign totalitarian states. It is the existence within our own personal attitudes and within our own institutions of conditions which have given a victory [to those foreign totalitarian states.] **The battlefield is also accordingly here – within ourselves and our institutions**. (John Dewey, *Freedom and Culture,* 1939)

> The most pressing constitutional question facing our country at this moment ... is whether we will abide by this clear command of the Fourteenth Amendment's disqualification clause. (Judge Michael Luttig, 2023)

To be clear, the summons issued here to our "U.S. House of Justice" is not just being delivered to our Department of Justice and our Courts of Justice, but is a summons to all the institutions of our self-government – including, but not limited to, the Congress, Supreme Court, Presidency, the 'fourth estate' of 'the Press,' and all our people-led organizations of civil society – which together make up the living Constitution that ALL of us, as patriotic members and elected or unelected officers of a government of, by, and for the people, are sworn "to support and defend ... against all enemies, foreign and domestic."

And therefore the purpose of the twin Indictments against our House of Justice issued here is to challenge all of us to work together to ensure that the overall outcome of our work together during 2024 results in rendering equal justice to all people in our country, including D.J. Trump, without fear or favor – in faithfulness to the most fundamental principle of our democratic Constitution, which is that **NO ONE is above the law.**

As Northrop Frye noted in light of the visionary truths of William Blake's poetry, such fundamental judgments – which could determine the historical fate of our nation in apocalyptic ways – cannot be "compelled" without igniting the imagination of the soul of a nation. And so the indictments rendered here are meant to awaken and ignite the imaginative vision of our national "House of Justice." These indictments are rendered as challenges in the hope that we can still come together to prevent the kind of slide into totalitarian fascism that German citizens witnessed in the early 1930s, and that many countries into recent days have been continuing to experience as once democratic governments and constitutions collapse under the determined assault of fascist leaders and their sycophantic supporters.

For in 2024, in the trials of D.J. Trump, the core judgments facing the nation beg the question: What are WE as a nation and a people showing ourselves to be as we put Trump on trial? Do we even know what we are doing? And if we do not clearly comprehend what we are doing, do we even begin to comprehend the existential and historical jeopardy in which we are placing the future of ALL of our lives as both a people and a nation when the continued existence of our democratic House of Justice is so fundamentally at risk?

Do we understand that the violent force of injustice we are facing in the person of Trump and the political movement supporting him is the contemporary force of a new monstrous birth of totalitarianism, which cannot be stopped by moral entreaties or weak, disorganized political moves? Do we understand that such a determined force of injustice *can only be stopped by the full application of the strongest and most lucid countervailing FORCE of Law and political action* rendered by a fully conscious (rather than somnambulant) House of Justice?

A glaring example of the kind of somnambulant consent allowing Trump to continue to march us all to the noose of our own destruction is the tortured avoidance of any commitment to action by Colorado's Denver District Court Judge Sarah B. Wallace who, after finding that Trump had indeed "engaged in insurrection," then pathetically betrayed the Constitutional authority given her and all judges by the disqualification clause of the 14th Amendment. Based on this clause of our Constitution, which is not intended to be a suicide pact, the judge had the authority to declare Trump to be disqualified to run for any political office in the state of Colorado.

Judge Wallace summarized: "the Court concludes ... that Trump incited an insurrection on Jan. 6, 2021 and therefore 'engaged' in insurrection within the meaning of Section 3 of the 14th Amendment." But then beyond reason, as if under the spell of some mind-deadening hypnosis, the judge went on to state that "the Court is persuaded that 'officers of the United States' did not include the President of the United States." In other words, according to Judge Wallace – even though the president is required to take the presidential Oath of Office that binds him just like any other federal office holder to defend the Constitution of the United States, and furthermore binds the holder of the Office of the presidency to "faithfully execute the OFFICE of President of the United States" – yet (according to Wallace) the person who takes the Presidential Oath of Office and swears to "faithfully execute the Office of President of the United States" is somehow not an "officer of the United States"?

Fortunately, this failure of judgment by the Denver District Court judge was over-ruled by the Colorado State Court, whose decision is now being reviewed by the Supreme Court of the United States, which now gives it the opportunity to reveal to all the world whether it too will FAIL to render a judgment that fulfills its responsibility to defend our Constitution from the existential threat facing it. To the extent that Trump's primary goal ever since at least 2020 has been to overthrow the principles of our Constitution, and has been enabled to continue to move inexorably toward this goal by the sycophantic assistance of the GOP and other appointed officers of his former and future administration (as "Project 2025" has so clearly outlined), this alone represents, in the words of David Rothkopf (in his book Traitor) "a profound betrayal" of our constitutional order.

Far from seeking to "preserve, protect and defend the Constitution of the United States" according to his Oath of Office, Trump's leading ambition has become the overthrow of all constitutional limitations on his power to use the Office of the presidency to serve his own corrupt interests. Yet even after coming to the now obvious conclusion that Trump "engaged in insurrection," our Courts and political leaders seem too enfeebled to step forward to enforce the action **demanded of us** by the Constitution, which is to disqualify a corrupt, 2x impeached, 4x criminally indicted insurrectionist from running for the highest office of the land to become the most powerful political "officer of the United States."

The definition of "Traitor," as David Rothkopf has explicated, is "one who betrays a trust or duty," as in an oath; or literally, "one who delivers, or hands over," from which we derive the application of the term "traitor" to one who sells out their nation by handing over secrets that betray the most fundamental trust invested by the people of the United States in the highest OFFICER of their government. The president of the United States takes an OATH of OFFICE that explicitly embodies the most fundamental duty of the President of the United States to "faithfully execute the OFFICE of President of the United States," and to "preserve, protect and defend the Constitution of the United States." So the fact that the Denver District Court judge could on one hand acknowledge that Trump had clearly "engaged in insurrection," and yet refuse to ACT on the clear command of the constitution to disqualify the insurrectionist from being able to run for political office, speaks all the more loudly to the ways ALL the leaders of our current weak and faltering House of Justice seem to be bending over backwards to avoid doing their duty to defend our Constitution from the destructive depredations – past, present, and future – so clearly committed and projected by D.J. Trump. Will the Officers of the Supreme Court now similarly fail to execute their duty?

This historical "summons" is therefore addressed to the U.S. "House of Justice" – comprised of the institutions of Congress, the Courts, the Presidency, the "Fourth Estate" of the Press/Media, and ultimately "the People Themselves," who are responsible for overseeing and determining the character of these institutions in a democratic Republic – as both a warning and an indictment of the ways we have so far failed to live up to our most fundamental obligation as citizens of a democratic Republic to ensure that "justice be done." And this failure of our entire House of Justice pertains not only narrowly to our indecisive action toward criminal Trump himself, but even more importantly toward the fascist movement of Trumpism seeking to overthrow our Republic – for "no tyrant maintains himself by force [alone], but by trading on his victims' fears," and "tyranny is seldom imposed on people from without; it is a projection of their own pusillanimity."

*****

Today as ever, we are charged with the present realization of the possible. This helps to determine the future, without our planning it. *We cannot expect what we do not help to achieve. What we fail to do today is lost forever*. (Karl Jaspers,

"Liberty and Authority," *Philosophy and the World,*
1963)

This *Summons* to the American people and our House of Justice is therefore a fundamental call to our Nation to live up to its highest ideals of justice in 2024, since our failure to do so will condemn us all to the loss of our democratic constitution. *This fundamental summons to Justice has two essential phases: an indictment of our ongoing Failures to live up to our ideals of Justice, and a call to Awakening and Action.*

First and foremost, this Summons is meant to call attention to, and deliver, a clear indictment of the already horribly evident failures of our House of Justice throughout 2023 – an indictment of its failures to uphold the most fundamental principles of justice: ***that all are equal before the law, and that no one is above the law*** in the United States. In our constant failures to act decisively (even in the most basic of ways by imposing firm protective gag orders as would have been employed against any other American under criminal indictment) in the face of Trump's continuing and perpetual incitements to intimidation and violence – which have never stopped since his speech before the Capitol on 1/6/2021 – our House of Justice has miserably failed to hold Trump accountable to the same rules of justice and human decency that every other person in the country would be held to.

These failures to hold Trump accountable to the rule of law seem to be occurring, in part, out of some grossly misguided and rationally unsound attempt to give honorific deference to a four-times criminally indicted man simply because he was a former president who is now running for president again. And this deference continues to govern the treatment of Trump throughout our political universe – even within portions of the Democratic Party – even though it has become evident that Trump is running for office with the explicitly avowed purpose of protecting himself from legal consequences for his past crimes along with the promise of taking a wrecking ball to our House of Justice in a way that would obliterate the warning inscribed into the limestone walls of the headquarters of the U.S. Department of Justice:

"Where law ends, tyranny begins."

Instead of enforcing the basic principle of any self-respecting modern organization, which is that its leaders should exemplify the standards of conduct expected of all its members, this honorific deference to Trump being demonstrated throughout our House of Justice suggests that as a people and a nation we no longer expect even our highest leaders in the Presidency (or Congress) to uphold ANY standards of integrity or responsibility. We seem completely willing to allow, even in the face of our Constitution's clear command for disqualification of insurrectionists, Trump to run for president a third time, even after he has so thoroughly demonstrated his complete lack of merit for any public office. Such willingness to allow this Trump Show to continue to dominate our political life boggles the mind of anyone who seeks to honor and respect our constitutional principles of justice, and suggests that the governing spirit of leadership in our country has descended into the kind of bottomless nihilistic pit that paves the way for totalitarian dictatorship.

Why are our judges and courts of justice seeming to go out of their way to grant special privileges or exceptions (that seem to place him "above the law") to a man who has perpetually disgraced the basic principles of leadership by using his "free speech" to defy and betray every common principle of human decency and law? Would any other person under criminal indictment in the United States, not to mention any other candidate running for political office while charged with 92 crimes, be allowed to so flagrantly disregard the rules imposed on other criminal defendants? If our House of Justice has already become so weak and depraved that it does not recognize the fundamental self-betrayal it is enacting every day it allows Trump to continue to defy the rules of law that would have thrown any other American behind bars months ago, ***then our House of Justice is already grievously lost, even before the trials of Trump begin in 2024.***

The twin Indictments rendered here (re: *our political failures of imagination and action*) are therefore directed at the sources of this terrible self-betraying weakness, which have opened our democratic Republic to collapse from within. For the triumph of totalitarian fascism "demands that the tortured victim allow himself to be led to the noose without protesting, that he renounce and abandon himself to the point of ceasing to affirm his identity."

*****

> We as citizens need to recognize [those ideas] that
> are essential to the preservation of that which is
> best about our system of government. None is more
> central to these than this idea of ensuring that no
> one is above the law. It is the reason the country
> was established, the reason we rejected the British
> monarchy and the rule of George III. (David
> Rothkopf, *Traitor* [2020], 209)

Secondly, this writing summons our U.S. House of Justice to an awakening from its somnambulant march toward the gallows of a national and world-historical apocalypse the likes of which we have not seen since the reins of the German government were placed in Hitler's hands in January of 1933.

This is a summons to our House of Justice in all of its institutional manifestations, as well as to the souls of the American people whose votes in November 2024 will be the ultimate determinant of whether or not this new monstrous birth of totalitarianism is allowed to overthrow all that justice and truth mean in our fragile human country and world. For if the most fundamental powers for constituting the justice of our politics and political institutions are surrendered into the hands of this new tyrant by the weakness of our responses to the totalitarian injustice already so clearly evident in the words and deeds of Trump and his movement – whether by incomprehension, or deliberate allowance of the subversion of the means of justice – then even before the elections of 2024 occur, the failed trials of Trump, just like the pivotal failed trial of Adolf Hitler 100 years ago, will inscribe into our history the spiritual failure of our politics and institutions of justice to rise to the challenge of defending our world from the totalitarian threat now campaigning to overthrow our constitutional order.

If we together allow our House of Justice to fail in rendering strict justice to Trump during 2024, if we the people allow our House of Justice to fail in its core mission of rendering equal justice to all under the principle that no one is above the law, we will have already failed to protect our nation from the clearly intended constitutional overthrow that Trump and his House of Injustice have projected onto our future. And in that failure, IF WE ALLOW IT, we the people and our institutions of justice will have become complicit in the suicide of our constitutional order of government not only at the federal level, but in school boards, towns, cities and states all across the nation. As Supreme Court

Justice Robert H. Jackson stated in 1949, Our constitution is not meant to be a suicide pact!

The immodest purpose of this writing is therefore to summon forth an imaginative spiritual and political awakening of our U.S. House of Justice to the perils and opportunities we – as a people and a nation – face in the prosecution of the Trump trials of 2024 as we move toward our November elections. This indictment of the current soul of our American "House of Justice" – which so far appears to be sleepwalking itself toward the apocalyptic end of our Republic as it continues to ALLOW the fraudulent Trump Show to dominate our national political stage – is meant to act like the shock of a lightning bolt that lands next to us and triggers a fundamental awakening of our political perspective and mode of political action.

We clearly need such a transformation of the spirit governing our House of Justice, since up to now the completely unimaginative attempts to limit the corrupting power of the Trump Show by such means as weak "gag orders" have proved utterly impotent. Such legal and political weakness in the face of a tyrant only provoke the totalitarian hyena to ever more vicious biting and howling attacks on those who threaten its ability to continue to do as it wills. And this kind of impotent legal response to the totalitarian campaigning of a wannabe dictator should remind us all of the utterly ludicrous 1924 response to the Hitler insurrection, which opened wide the doors to the ultimate destruction of the German democratic republic.

As we contemplate the disastrous failures of the past to respond appropriately to the threat of a rising fascism, we should hold clearly in mind the recent declarations from our few bold and courageous Dorothies who over the past two years have, like Dorothy in the Wizard of Oz, pulled back the curtain on the orange clown-wizard manipulating the levers of power that keep the munchkins in fearful obedience:

As E. Jean Carroll has declared, **"Trump is nothing... He's not even there. We don't need to be afraid of him."** And like Cassidy Hutchinson who has so directly put to shame the whole Republican party of male sycophants allowing fear to determine their ring-kissing relationship to Trump, we must all challenge every political leader in the country to shout just as clearly as Hutchinson did, in Trump's face: "Enough!"

*****

> The victory over all kinds of authoritarian systems will be possible only if democracy does not retreat but takes the offensive and proceeds to realize what has been its aim in the minds of those who fought for freedom throughout the last centuries. (Erich Fromm, *Escape from Freedom*, 1941)

In the scathing introduction to her analysis of the failures of the Eichmann trial to live up to the dictates of strict justice, Hannah Arendt addressed one of the fundamental flaws that weakened the outcome of that historic 1961 trial: "There is no doubt from the very beginning that it is Judge Landau who sets the tone, and that he is doing his best, his very best, to prevent this trial from becoming a 'show trial' under the prosecutor's love of showmanship" (4).

Similarly, in the trials of Trump, if the institutions of justice responsible for protecting the administration of justice do not do their duty to restrain and dismantle the ability of the Trump Show to continue to manipulate and distort the purpose of these trials, we will be faced with the spectacle, throughout the trials of 2024, of watching in shocked frustration as the judges and prosecutors charged with overseeing these trials struggle to do "their best, their very best," to prevent every one of these trials from descending into the realm of farcical show trials under chief criminal defendant Trump's "love of showmanship."

The question we must all be asking ourselves as we respond to developments in 2024 is therefore: ***Will the U.S. House of Justice wake up from the somnambulance that continued to hobble its efforts to protect itself from the gathering force of tyranny throughout 2023, and rise up to embody the courage of clear action in the face of the historic challenges 2024 will demand of us?*** OR will the U.S. House of Justice prove itself to be as weak and incompetent as was the German House of Justice when faced with the 1924 trial of the man and the movement that had already made clear its intent to destroy that Republic?

When the institutions and words of law are lucidly awake and focused strictly on what is necessary to fulfill their core ethico-political task in a democracy – to render equal justice to all without fear or favor – these institutions, and the words used to render justice, can be powerful instruments in the defense of democracy. But when we the people allow our institutions and the language of law to lose their way and get caught up in the distortions of partisan politics, and even worse in the distortions of political campaigning, these very institutions and the language of law itself – which at their best can serve as the bulwark of a constitutional democracy – can utterly fail and thereby become core instruments of a democracy's demise. When the language and "wordiness" of law is allowed to become an impediment to the strict prosecution of justice, it can be transformed into the unwilling or willing tool of the worst kinds of injustice, as the progressive degradations of law in totalitarian Germany so clearly showed us during the 1930s.

In 2024, as the people of the United States face an historic crisis not unlike that of pre-Nazi Germany in the early 1930s, only we the people can determine which of these two destinies our U.S. House of Justice will fulfill, to the salvation or perdition of our political and spiritual nation. Let us all work together to ensure that OUR institutions of justice do not fail to hold our tyrant accountable to the rule of law and justice in 2024.

I.

Indictments Rendered against the U.S. House of Justice (All of Us)

No authority more useful and necessary can be granted to those appointed to look after the liberties of a state than that of being able to indict before the people or some magistrate or court such citizens as have committed any offence prejudicial to the freedom of the state... For fear of being prosecuted, its citizens attempt nothing prejudicial to the state, and, if they do attempt anything, are suppressed forthwith without respect to persons. (Machiavelli, *The Discourses [on Livy]* I.7, "How Necessary Public Indictments are for the Maintenance of Liberty in a Republic")

I. Twin Indictments Rendered Against the U.S. "House of Justice"

The most fundamental question posed here by the following two indictments of our U.S. "House of Justice" is this:

Are "We the People" of the United States going to allow ourselves to be marched to the gallows and hung by the noose of Trumpism without a fight? If so, it will be the second time in modern history a nation will have so willingly and deliberately surrendered its existence as a Republic to its own declared destroyer – without much more than a whimper of protest!

Such an abject surrender, after the hard lessons learned from the history of Nazi Germany, is absolutely disgusting to contemplate. And yet this is precisely what now appears to be happening here, as a sleepwalking nation allows a proven tyrant who has sworn himself to the destruction of our constitutional republic to run for the highest office of the land for a third time, as if our nation with all the power of its institutions is paralyzed to do anything about it!

WHY?

> We are fighting totalitarianism in behalf of
> freedom… The fight is a struggle for freedom within
> the free countries. It would become senseless if we
> were to lose at home what we are trying to defend
> from outside attack… More and more distinctly it
> comes to be a showdown with ourselves. We may
> hope that it will be waged with clear vision and
> acute intelligence in the concrete situations. It is in
> this task that our forces meet or split or grow
> confused on the plain basic issue of our spiritual
> fate, and of its consequences in political reality.
> (Karl Jaspers, "The Fight Against Totalitarianism,"
> *Philosophy and the World*, 1963)

As noted above, "when we the people allow our institutions and the language of law to lose their way and get caught up in the distortions of partisan politics, and even worse in the distortions of political campaigning, these very institutions and the language of law itself – which at their best can serve as the bulwark of a constitutional democracy – fail and thereby become core instruments of a democracy's demise."

What does this mean, exactly, for understanding the core responsibilities facing the American people as we impatiently await the long-delayed beginning of the criminal trials of D.J. Trump in 2024? Or, in other words, what is at stake for understanding our core responsibilities as democratic citizens of a republic in 2024?

In short, if we do not clearly distinguish our political responsibilities from our more limited legal responsibilities for defending the U.S. House of Justice, and thereby acknowledge the responsibilities we all have to take appropriate action to protect our constitutional Republic, there is nothing the trials of D.J. Trump can do to save us and our Republic. If we fail as a political nation to uphold our Constitution from attack, then we cannot rely on the courts of justice alone to protect us from the consequences of the breach in our constitutional defenses opened up by our larger political failure to act to end the fascist movement that threatens our entire constitutional structure.

The foundation of the following two indictments against our U.S. House of Justice (which includes all of us) is clear recognition of our failure to act politically over the last three years to stop the Trump Show from continuing its totalitarian march to power through the abuse, and projected overthrow, of our constitutional norms and institutions. And because of that fundamental failure, the political risk of the Trump trials of 2024 is that they, just like the Hitler trial of 1924, will become an integral part of fueling the continuing development of the Trump political campaign and the fascist movement supporting it, which our political inaction has so far allowed to continue to gather strength.

The nature of a fascist movement is that it absorbs everything into itself, including all attempts of a justice system to interdict it when the political and constitutional systems have proven themselves too weak to stop the ongoing development of the fascist movement. If decisive political action is not taken, and our political nation fails to act constitutionally - using the power bestowed on it by the 14th Amendment - to prevent declared insurrectionists from taking control of the government, then all merely legal attempts to do so through the court system will be burdened with a weight they cannot carry by themselves. In the face of such political failure, our court-based system of justice is likely to collapse under this weight, due to the betrayal of the courts by the rest of the constitutional political system, which has so far failed to hold up its end of the constitutional bargain to protect the rule of law from being undermined politically by a totalitarian movement dedicated precisely to that aim.

First Indictment: *Our Failure to Think Creatively*

> What does mark [totalitarian rule] is the principle of the lie. Truth and falsehood, reality and fiction, are so blended that the outcome is not illumination but the reality of the radical lie... What is specific in totalitarianism is the basic tendency and its extreme form: the lie is a cardinal principle of totalitarian doctrine. (Karl Jaspers, "Freedom and Totalitarianism," *The Future of Mankind*, 1963)

The U.S. House of Justice has so far failed to *think imaginatively* about what citizens of a democracy can do to effectively "support and defend the Constitution of the United States against all enemies, foreign and domestic."

We call ourselves a "democratic" nation, but do so unthinkingly, without even asking ourselves whether we have a clue as to what that means. In fact, by our failure so far to confront and terminate the Trump Show and its fascist political movement, we have demonstrated that in the current moment of our democracy's existential crisis we simply don't understand what it means to be in the spiritual character of the kind of "citizen" of a "democracy" who knows what to do to effectively join together with fellow citizens to fight for and defend democracy against a fascist assault on our constitution. We seem to lack the political imagination to think our way through to a clear understanding of what we all should be doing to work in a clearly organized and strategic way to preserve our democracy from being destroyed by the totalitarian form of fascist movement represented by Trumpism.

And through our failures of thinking and acting in response to the corruptions of Trumpism, we all are instead marching like dummies to the noose of the destruction of our Republic. Why is this? What is the root cause of our nation's abject victimization by the continuing plague of the Trump Show and the horrible political farce of its Big Lies, due to our failures to act politically to end this fascist threat to our constitutional existence?

Our somnambulant thinking and apparent inability to imagine a different political reality is in part due to our complacency over the supposed permanence and inevitability of our much-vaunted democratic Republic. And our illusion of living in a "democratic" Republic that, as President Biden all-too-glibly states is the "necessary" nation to the rest of the world - as if we have some divinely preordained right to a continued existence, and cannot imagine the end of this current reality - is no doubt due in part to the power that simple numbers exercise over our imagination.

We tell ourselves we're a nation of some 340 million people and live in a democracy that has survived over 240 years, and assume we'll be celebrating our country's semiquincentennial (250th anniversary) in 2026. But what if our Constitution has been effectively nullified by 2026? After Hitler was handed the reins of federal power in January 1933, it took him only 3 months to completely suspend both the German constitution and the German equivalent of Congress, the Reichstag, along with the judicial structures for defending the civil rights of German citizens. And with a man who has already declared his clear intention to act like a dictator on "Day One" of his next administration, do we have any basis for doubting that Trump's dismantling of our constitutional system of checks and balances will not occur as swiftly as Hitler's?

Given our long-established power in the world, along with our long-established history (since in an age when history is no longer valued, let alone studied and understood, 250 years can be confused with eternity), we assume that since our country has survived for so long it must inevitably continue to do so. And in pursuit of our self-involved and narrowly conceived sense of political responsibility, we continue to make unthinking political judgments, based on mere numbers, even in the direct face of how close we came to the immediate dissolution of our Republic in the 245th year of its existence on 1/6/2021, when the long uninterrupted chain of the peaceful transfer of power from one President to the next was suddenly broken by Trump's insurrectionary assault on the Capitol!

Now I have not the least doubt that most of us (excepting those who have sacrificed their souls to the golden calf of Trumpism) are honest enough, when by ourselves, to say in our solitary conversations something like: "If I'm honest with myself, I don't deny that I've avoided taking up the responsibilities of being a "citizen" in the true sense of that term. And if I'm brutally honest, I can't deny that my life cannot be called even an effort in the direction of what true citizenship requires of us as individuals, especially in the direction of giving up some of my self-seeking pursuits to offer service to strengthen our democratic institutions and 'preserve, protect and defend' the constitutional life of the Republic."

And I have no doubt that most of us (except those who have corrupted their souls to the point of not being able to distinguish between truth and lie even in the most sacred space of their own souls, which space has been rendered a wasteland by a self-abnegating subjection to the lies of Trumpism) will admit, as I have, that we have not lived up to the true ideals of citizenship, and that we have, for the most part, not yet succeeded in restructuring our lives in the direction of becoming true citizens worthy of a democratic Republic.

And yet as soon as we leave the space of our solitary dialogue with ourselves, and rejoin the public dialogue of millions of our fellow so-called "citizens," we quickly become confused by the common tropes of our self-excusing and unthinking political language, since aren't all of us, after all, citizens in a democratic Republic? The indictment - here - of "all of us," is meant to challenge every single one of us to stop and think long enough to truly ask ourselves this single question, as part of a process of shaking ourselves out of our zombified unthinking state:

Are we living in our power as democratic citizens? Or do we each embody, in the daily political avoidances of our lives, everything that betrays the existential reality of what true citizenship demands of us, especially in historical moments like the one we are living thru now, where the entire existence of democracy is at stake in a tortured country like the United States? Do we know what citizenship means, or what it requires of us? Are we willing to THINK this question through, and then ACT on the results of our thinking?

For inasmuch as democratic citizenship involves spirit, and demands a sobriety of spirit that comes with the existential contemplation of eternity in "the instant" of apocalyptic crisis, there is nothing so suspicious to a self-critical detective eye as all the fantastic common phrases that in our current moment of crisis ooze from every pore of our national media and political discourse to comfort us in the sense that we are all, after all, citizens of a great republic. As we all are caught up in the hypnotic powers of the 24-hour media cycle that we continually collude with, and thereby fall into an unthinking collaboration with the prevailing media discourse, we become narcotized to protect ourselves and each other from being shocked into a sudden awakening to recognition of how terribly we are failing to live up to the core responsibilities of our citizenship!

For insofar as we each continue to collude with our common unthinking media discourse in the work of seeking to save each other from the shock of a needed awakening, by continual unthinking use of such phrases as "democratic state," "democratic people," or most amazingly of all the idea that we are citizens of a "democratic Republic," we are ALL guilty of actively participating in the propagation of the most fundamental "Big Lie" that governs our current moment of somnambulant national existence: the Big Lie that the terms "democratic" or "citizen," or for that matter even the term "freedom" have any meaningful reference to our current stupefied state of political existence.

In other words, it is our own failure to honestly recognize we have failed the test of living up to the challenges of democratic citizenship that has

opened the gates of the abyss out of which the monstrous tyranny of Trumpism and its fascist movement have arisen.

Under the current circumstances of our national political crisis, every time a phrase like "democratic country" is uttered without it being surrounded by scare quotes to underline its problematic status, a monstrous offense to "thinking" itself is being perpetrated. And everything our country has so far seen in the way of Trump's criminal offenses and Trumpism's Big Lies pales in comparison with these daily lies we tell each other every minute to maintain ourselves in the self-deceived spiritual condition of believing we are "citizens" living in a "democracy," while we continue to fail to fulfill any of the basic political responsibilities in the regular course of our lives that are required to make democracy or citizenship existential realities in the world.

It is this deeper Big Lie – that we are all colluding in propagating by our unwillingness to stop and think seriously about our current existential political situation – which has made it possible for the Big Lies of Trumpist fascism to make such fearful headway in our country over the last eight years due to the absence of any clear and spirited political counter-movement directed at attacking the political foundations of Trumpism. And it is our own failures to think imaginatively, and to hold ourselves accountable for living up to the challenge of the meaning of the words "citizenship" and "democracy," that have kept this effective political counter-movement from developing to defeat Trumpism.

And so therefore the first indictment of the U.S. House of Justice is this: We have all been colluding in the perpetuation of the unthinking discourse of the present moment that is unwilling to stop and think about what it means to be a true "citizen" of a "democratic" Republic. And through that most basic of collusions, we have all rendered ourselves passive enablers of the foundations of power (financial and institutional) that have made the propagation of the Big Lies of Trumpism possible. Through such collusion we have also disabled ourselves from being able to understand what we are required to do to interdict the coming destruction the Trump Show has prepared for our nation.

The continued facilitation of our marching like dummies to the noose of our own political apocalypse requires of us no more than a somnambulant consent to the unthinking political status quo, which assumes (without thinking) that the survival of our democratic republic is inevitable, and requires nothing out of the ordinary from us to continue its existence. Just like all our other consumer goods, our unthinking politics is thought to require nothing more than an occasional "purchase" (through casting a vote or making a financial contribution), after which we can continue our private pursuits without being bothered by thoughts about where our political future will come from since, after all, it will of course always be there waiting for us, as it always has been, world without end, Amen.

Until enough of us wake up from this political stupor, turn, and stop to begin thinking about the spiritual meanings of these words "citizen" and "democracy," and begin to challenge every one of our fellow citizens to the same responsibility for thinking, our Republic will continue to remain the victim of – and will continue to suffer under the deadening weight of – its spiritual submission to the propaganda of fear that is the dominating weapon of the Trumpist fascism driving our country toward the abyss of its own apocalypse in 2024.

First Indictment: The U.S. House of Justice has so far failed to think imaginatively about what citizens of a democracy can do to effectively "support and defend the Constitution of the United States against all enemies, foreign and domestic."

Second Indictment: *Our Failure to Act Decisively as Citizens*

The U.S. House of Justice has so far failed to act decisively to "support and defend the Constitution of the United States against all enemies, foreign and domestic" by dismantling the ongoing efforts of the Trumpist movement to attack and destroy our Republic.

This second indictment is one previously issued as part of the 2021 Introduction to a book dedicated to revealing what action was needed in 2022 to effectively resist and "Undo the Folded Lie of Trumpism." As a newly updated second edition of this book is being prepared for 2024, this current "Summons" is being added as Preface to further highlight the urgency of the previous "message in a bottle" dropped into the 2022 political sea of silence that greeted a book which challenged all Americans to wake up and act to put an end to the grifting Trump wizard show:

"The current moment of American political history is haunted by the imagery of the Wizard of Oz as our political parties and institutions have cowered in fear and inaction, allowing themselves to be dominated by the spectacle and discourse of an orange-faced clown and his propaganda of fear. Especially our GOP politicians, as the moral and political munchkins they are, have been cowering in fear before this faux wizard of Mar-a-Lago as if he is the master of the universe. And meanwhile, behind the scenes of this jury-rigged political show, for anyone like Dorothy who has the courage to dare to pull away the curtain, there is just a pathetic, fraudulent clown with fake orange hair, who is allowed to continue manipulating the levers of power through the propaganda of fear.

"The only reason this orange wizard continues to get away with his power game of manipulation is because we the people have collectively failed to summon the political will to stop him, not only by pulling away the curtain to expose him for the total fraud he is, but then also by acting [legally and politically] to pull him away from his levers of political and financial power as producer (with his co-conspirators) of the 'Trump Show,' by which he continues to use the propaganda of fear and the Big Lie to hold sway over the tens of millions of people who continue to support and fund his evil wizard show – including the vast majority of so-called 'leaders' and elected representatives of the once 'Grand Old Party' of President Lincoln who defended the Constitution and won a Civil War against exactly the likes of such traitors and sycophants as these."

Instead of acting decisively to pull the orange wizard away from the levers of power and funding that allow him to continue to produce the clown show of what has now become his third campaign for the Presidency of the United States, a somnambulant Republic of sleeping "citizens" – guided by its media and political establishment leaders, along with the willingly deluded masses (of tens of millions of our fellow "citizens") who directly fund and thereby continue to empower this fascist movement - choose to give their consent to the continuation of this fascist "Walpurgis Night" horror show that has made clear its ultimate intent of overthrowing our constitutional Republic.

And so, in the closing months of 2023, even after the unfolding of 4 separate criminal indictments of this fascist wizard and his criminal clown show, in all its fraudulent and sickening details, because no decisive action has yet been taken to shut down the political continuation of this Trump Show, our nation is allowing this orange wizard to continue to dominate our political reality even while the leadership of our country's political, legal, and media institutions continue to pretend they are powerless to escape its grasp or do anything about it – as if they lack all ability to imagine any alternative reality, and lack any creative means by which they could shut this fraudulent wizard show down. Thus, out of cowardice and sycophantic complacency, due to the twin failures to engage both political thinking and imagination, they all bow down before the power of this orange golem god they have made, and to whom they continue to provide the energy and funding to rule over them, all while professing to be "Christian" "citizens" of a "democracy"!

"This is the absurdist reality of the present moment in the United States under the rule of Trumpism and its perverse Trump Show. And this political clown show continues to dominate our reality only because our political and media leaders, as well as all of us who could demand change from these leaders, lack both the imagination and will of a truth-telling and truth-acting Dorothy to pull away the curtains protecting this Trump Show, and to stop the fraudulent activity of the evil orange wizard hiding behind these curtains of protection. And these curtains are continually fortified by the unthinking imaginations of the entire American republic that continues to muddle on as if there is nothing that could be done to arrest this Trump Show and shut it down!"

The ogre-wizard's most serious crime, detailed nowhere in any of the 4 criminal indictments rendered against him, but foundational to them all, is his so-far unhindered construction of a political world of lies that is shredding our shared world of human life, tearing to pieces the foundations of a constitution that binds us to each other in a functioning political world of civility and love. Yet so long as all we do is stand by and watch in horror, transfixed by the political nightmare the Trump Show is intended to produce, by being unwilling to stand up and walk out of the horrible show in protest, and then to do something to shut it down – so long as this inaction continues, we are all complicit in this show's continuation, and in whatever disastrous results it renders for our country and our common human history beyond 2024.

And so this second indictment against the U.S. House of Justice is not only an indictment of the cowardly, sycophantic complacency of the leaders of the G.O.P. who are the immediate propagators and supporters of the Trump Show, but is also an indictment of the entire American public for failing to stand up to take action and demand that their political leaders shut down this Trump horror show once and for all, before it is too late:

Second Indictment: Even as you have issued four criminal indictments against Trump, you have failed to take decisive action to shut down the Trump Show that is determined to end our Republic. The U.S. House of Justice has therefore failed to act decisively to "support and defend the Constitution of the United States against all enemies, foreign and domestic" by dismantling the ongoing efforts of the Trumpist movement to attack and destroy our Republic.

II.

Argument:
The "Facts of the Case"

II. Argument: the "Facts of the Case"

The body of the argument in any legitimate trial in the eyes of the law (as opposed to a fraudulent form of trial, which is ultimately a kind of lie, most infamously a form of "show trial" where the semblance of the trial form and the language of justice is utilized as a façade for propagating a predetermined story or judgment, independent of fact or evidence, based simply on the pre-formed prejudices or political objectives of the "producers" of the show trial) is directed at providing specific proofs, based on clear evidence, for validating the truth of the claims made in the indictments, in order to provide a firm foundation for the concluding judgments that constitute the verdicts rendered by the trial.

In her candid critique of the weaknesses of the Eichmann trial, Hannah Arendt pointed out that "there is no doubt from the very beginning that it [was] Judge Landau who sets the tone, and that he [was] doing his best, his very best, to prevent this trial from becoming a show trial under the prosecutor's love of showmanship" (Eichmann in Jerusalem, 4). Arendt's core critique of the defects of this historical trial, in so far as it failed to accomplish its chief objective of simply ensuring that "justice be seen to be done" to Eichmann, was that the Judge's intent to ensure justice was constantly undermined by a "show trial" political prosecutor who was working to bring into the trial a whole world of evidence that distracted and obscured the central through-line of evidence directly relevant to the indictment at hand and to the specific judgment that needed to be rendered to make it possible for a public audience to clearly "see" that justice was done, without being confused by a whole range of other motivations and lessons that, however well-intended, would end up interfering with the clear prosecution of justice.

According to Arendt, one of the chief defects of the Eichmann trial was that the Judge was put in the position of single-handedly having to guard the purpose of the trial – as a vehicle for delivering justice – from the dangerous obfuscations of the prosecutor's "love of showmanship," which was constantly working to turn the trial into a show case for pre-scripted and, as Arendt argues, largely superfluous or dangerously misleading "lessons" of history that often had no direct relevance to the facts of the case concerning what Eichmann had actually done.

In the case of our Trump trials, it is clear that the Judges in each of the four cases are also being put in the extremely uncomfortable position of having to do their "very best" to prevent all four trials from descending into the spectacle of show trials – not due to the "love of showmanship" by the prosecutors, as in the Eichmann trial, but due to the overmastering political "showmanship" of chief defendant Trump and his numerous public supporters in both the Congressional and media realms who can be considered the co-producers, with the chief defendant, of what we are designating the "Trump Show."

Indeed, just as Judge Landau did his "very best" to combat the showmanship of the chief prosecutor in the Eichmann trial, it's clear that in the Trump criminal cases before us – as was demonstrated by the way the Trump Show attempted to interfere with the prosecution of his civil trials – it will be the "showmanship" of the chief defendant and his supporters, rather than of the prosecutors, that the Judges are constantly having to battle and guard against.

Unlike the Eichmann trial, the prosecutors for the Trump trials have so far shown themselves to be aligned with the trial judges (except for the questionable case of Trump-appointed and possibly corrupt Judge Cannon) in working to ensure the strict accountability of each trial and its procedures to the specific evidence supporting the indictment of the defendants for what they have done, not for what they have said (since the prosecutors have gone out of the way to acknowledge that Trump has First Amendment speech rights to be honored just like every other defendant). The Trump indictments themselves have clearly ruled out any focus on a whole host of related issues and evidence that could be drawn from the long list of Trump's other criminal liabilities stemming from his two impeachments and the Mueller investigation. While the Judges, the U.S. Department of Justice, prosecutor Jack Smith and the state prosecutors are therefore doing their "very best" to focus carefully on the requirements of justice, the volume of noise and distraction constantly being produced by chief defendant Trump and his Clown Show of public defenders in Congress and beyond, are making this objective very difficult.

The fact that nothing is being done by our other political institutions and the media to shut down the ongoing drama of the "Trump Show" is placing not only these trial judges and prosecutors, but all our institutions of justice, in an extremely tenuous position. The political noise of the Trump Show campaign is in fact making it very difficult for our entire constitutional House of Justice to focus directly and simply on the requirements of doing justice so long as the stage manager of the Trump Show is allowed to continue to operate freely to mis-represent the significance of every step in trial preparation, even before the trials begin. Add to this the Trump Show's attack-dog efforts to threaten and intimidate everyone from witnesses to jury pool candidates by a constant barrage of Big Lie propaganda intended to undermine the very capacity of our system to conduct a "fair trial" by a citizen jury.

With this central challenge in mind, let us now focus on unfolding the argument and evidence that validates the truth of the claims set forth in the above two indictments, with specific reference to the four Trump trials that are at least still scheduled to take place throughout 2024, in spite of all the ongoing efforts of the

Trump Show to delay their prosecution until after the November election.

Since the outcomes of these four trials will either empower our national struggles to defeat Trumpism in the 2024 elections, or disempower our ability to defeat Trumpism through the nullification of the force of justice accomplished by the productions of the Trump Show, it is absolutely critical that all Americans concerned about the future of our Republic work to become lucidly clear about our public duties, as citizens, in regard to these trials. That is, if we want to claim the title of being "citizens" instead of just spectators watching 2024 play itself out as a horror show of national self-delusion and democratic impotence.

In considering this argument, therefore, each reader as judge must keep clearly in mind the single most important question before us all, to understand the full import of these two indictments, which is: What must each of us do, as a true citizen of a democratic Republic, to ensure that the outcomes of these trials, and the judgments they render on the criminal acts of Donald J. Trump, are not nullified by the continuing productions of the Trump Show?

Will we allow these trials to be reduced to merely distracting "show trials" incorporated as episodes into the overarching production of the Trump Campaign Show throughout 2024? And therefore, will we allow the trials to take place as mere distractive entertainment for us while we allow our nation to be marched to the gallows of our own political apocalypse?

OR, will we act politically as citizens together to defend our constitutional order of justice so that these trials are protected from, and guarded against the politics of the Trump Show, so that the verdicts of criminal justice can be rendered without the otherwise inevitable interference of the insurrectionist political theatrics Trump will ensure the trials and their verdicts are subjected to, just as Hitler did in his 1924 trial a hundred years ago? For as long as Trump is allowed to continue to campaign for the Presidency, he and his followers will be working constantly to transform and integrate the publicity generated by these trials into propaganda for the Trump Show campaign. And if we allow this to happen, our House of Justice will be allowing Trump – just like the Munich government allowed Hitler – to use these trials as platforms for furthering their fascist movement's campaign.

While the history of 2021-2023 will be written as one of failure to adequately take up the tools of our constitutional self-defense to ensure the Trump Show would not continue to be a national security threat, 2024 does not have to be a continuation of this process of failure if our House of Justice learns to stand up and fight to defend itself, our Constitution, and our Republic against this clearly announced coming dictatorship.

So now the only question is: Will 2024 be the year we reverse this ongoing surrender by standing up our House of Justice to fight, or will 2024 culminate the destruction of our Constitution as our House of Justice willingly surrenders itself to be walked to the Trumpist gallows prepared for it?

The argument related to these twinned indictments is therefore meant to highlight the ultimate significance of the potentially apocalyptic "stage setting" our somnambulant House of Justice has prepared for the Trump trials. The argument below is intended to provide a critical perspective that summons all Americans as true citizens to watch, analyze, and judge how the pivotal year of 2024 will play out, depending on what we each do to ensure our Constitutional system of government is adequately defended:

Either our House of Justice will continue to sleepwalk and allow the Trump Show to continue to control and manipulate our national political stage, which will end up making a mockery of all our best legal efforts to render justice as the Trump Show continues to progress toward its projected overthrow of our Constitution; OR our House of Justice – through our empowered action as democratic citizens – will WAKE UP to its mission and summon all its creative force to put down the Trump Show, and in so doing work to re-establish the meaning and foundations of our democratic Republic based on the principles of equal justice for all, without fear of, or favor to, the wealthy, powerful, or tyrannical.

Argument re: First Indictment – *Our Failure to Think Imaginatively*

The U.S. House of Justice has so far failed to think imaginatively about what citizens of a democracy can do to effectively "support and defend the Constitution of the United States against all enemies, foreign and domestic" through implementation of the 3rd Clause of the 14th Amendment.

Question: What is needed to implement an alternative to the continued domination of our politics by, and our continued political subjection to, the Trump Show?

Apart from conservative Judge Michael Luttig, no one on the national stage since the summer of 2022 has so vividly underlined our most foundational failures of imagination related to our difficulty with taking up the power directly gifted to us by the 3rd Clause of the 14th Amendment to defend our Constitution from the continuing threats of insurrectionists running for high political office. The essential tool is there, yet for lack of imagination our politicians, judges, citizens, and Supreme Court Justices have been slow to take this tool in hand to creatively apply it to the purpose for which it was given to us by those who survived the insurrectionists of the Civil War, and hoped to protect the nation from having to go through a similar experience again. And because we have been so slow to use our political imaginations to apply that tool to the task at hand, we have continued to suffer under our continued subjection to the Trump Show.

Imagine the counter-factual of a historical development over the last three years where, as soon as the insurrection occurred, the courts, our best legal minds, our political leaders, and our media had united to pull together a strategy, based on the 14th Amendment, to clearly and conclusively determine that Trump would be ineligible to run for President of the United States in 2024 or any other year. That simple determination, submitted to judicial review, and ultimately signed off on by the U.S. Supreme Court by mid-2023, would have relegated all the noise and bluster of the Trump Show over the last two years to the fringes of our political life, where the existing institutions for defending justice and upholding the law against those who resort to violence are at their strongest. And with that decisive action in defense of our Constitution and House of Justice, Trump would not have been able to run for President of the United States in 2024.

Instead, by the collective failure of our House of Justice to make this clear determination to take action by 2022, based on Constitutional law and the employment of our democratic political imaginations to implement a constitutional clause not used since the end of the Civil War, we are in the present predicament of extreme crisis, at serious risk of losing our entire constitutional democracy to an acknowledged insurrectionist and declared wannabe dictator.

In our collective failure to think and act differently in the decisive three years after the January 2021 Insurrection, we have all colluded in the perpetuation of the unthinking discourse of the present moment that is unwilling to stop and think about what it means to be a true "citizen" of a "democratic" Republic. And until enough of us turn around to stop and begin thinking about the spiritual meaning of these words "citizen" and "democratic," our Republic will continue to be victimized by the propaganda of fear that is the ruling weapon of the fascism driving our country toward the abyss of its own apocalypse in 2024.

So – if we are not willing to continue to allow ourselves "to be led to the noose like dummies without protesting," and to somnambulantly embrace the dissolution of our identities, we must learn to think differently. Since this first indictment concerns our apparent failure to imagine a strategy for overcoming the status quo of our continued subjection to the violence of the Trump Show, how do we begin to think differently about our current predicament? Indeed, how do we finally begin to think imaginatively about our current political crisis?

First, we must understand that beginning to think differently is the first step toward imaginatively comprehending what we need to do to develop the will to act to end our subservience to the Trump Show that is driving us toward a constitutional apocalypse. We must accept our responsibility to summon the power of our political imaginations to change our modes of thinking about what we need to do to ACT differently.

In The Atlantic Summer 2023 article titled "The Constitution Prohibits Trump from Ever Being President Again," Judge Luttig and Laurence Tribe set out their argument for the simple and direct application of the 14th Amendment disqualification clause to our current predicament. Since there is clear evidence of Trump's participation in an insurrection already provided in the 2021 impeachment hearing, the indictments of Jack Smith, and the evidentiary hearings before the Courts in Colorado, in addition to what we all witnessed during the day of January 6, 2021 and in the years since then, there is little reason to doubt the relevance of the 3rd clause of the 14th Amendment to Trump's case due to the multiple ways in which he attempted to keep himself in power in direct defiance of constitutional standards of presidential conduct.

Since Trump failed to uphold his Presidential Oath of Office to preserve and defend the Constitution while he was in office, and since then has made horribly clear his intent to overthrow the basic structures of the Constitution if he ever gets back into office, there is no reasonable standard by which this constitutionally self-protective clause would not apply to him, unless we want to embrace the notion that our Constitution is a suicide pact.

And as Judge Luttig summarized his argument on MSNBC's "Deadline Whitehouse" with Nicole Wallace on 11/5/23:

"The most pressing constitutional question facing our country at this moment ... is whether we will abide by this clear command of the Fourteenth Amendment's disqualification clause" to address Trump's clear and grave crimes of insurrection committed against the U.S. Constitution. As Luttig argues, no legal conviction of insurrection is necessary for disqualification since this clause makes it clear that – like other disqualifying reasons articulated by the Constitution, such as age or being foreign-born – having participated in an insurrection is automatically disqualifying. According to Luttig, Section 3 is "self-executing" as a matter of definition for what qualifies or disqualifies any candidate from office. The Constitution tells us that it is the conduct that gives rise to disqualification. Therefore in order to be eligible for federal or state political office, you cannot have participated in insurrection against the Constitution of the United States.

Trump is therefore by definition – through the evidence of both his acts and words –· disqualified from standing for federal office, and we the people and leaders of the institutions of the United States now need to do our duty to uphold and execute this requirement of the Constitution, just as we would for excluding any candidates from running for offices for which they did not meet the age or nationality requirements.

For all of us and our institutions to fail to uphold this requirement of the Constitution, just because this part of the Constitution has not been used since the nineteenth century, would be a fundamental failure of both the people and the institutions of the U.S. to exercise political imagination to "support and defend the Constitution of the United States" by following its direction and executing it's command. And "abiding by this clear command of the Fourteenth Amendment's disqualification clause" is critical not only in relation to Trump, but in relation to all the other state and federal office holders who disqualified themselves from office by supporting the insurrection of 1/6/2021 through providing aid and comfort to the enemies of our Constitution.

According to Luttig, it is Trump's clear attempt – through his documented participation in a coordinated plan to overturn the 2020 election results – to remain in office beyond the four years allowed him by the Constitution's Executive Vesting Clause, that defines his most fundamental act of defiance and insurrection against the Constitution. As Luttig notes, this is a "quintessential rebellion against the Constitution of the United States," which demands our response. Our failure to act appropriately to execute and enforce this "clear command" of the Constitution in the face of a presidential plot to overthrow our Constitution, may be fatal to our constitutional survival as a Republic.

Argument re: Second Indictment – Our Failure to Act Decisively

The U.S. House of Justice has so far failed to act decisively to end our subjection to the Trump Show and to "support and defend the Constitution of the United States against all enemies, foreign and domestic" by dismantling the ongoing efforts of the Trumpist movement to attack and destroy our democratic republic.

Question: Why have we failed to act decisively as citizens to Shut Down the Trump Show, and to end our subjection to the Trump Show so that we could appropriately defend our Constitution? What do we need to DO to End the Trump Show – by standing up to treat Trump, without fear or favor, the same as every other criminal defendant?

This second indictment is explicitly directed not only against the cowardly, sycophantic complacency of the leaders of the G.O.P. who are the immediate propagators and supporters of the Trump Show, but also against all of us who, as citizens of this Republic, continue to fail to stand up and take action to shut down the Trump horror show before it is too late! For even as our House of Justice has issued four criminal indictments against Trump, we have failed to take decisive action to shut down a Trump Show that is determined to delay, manipulate and corrupt any trials extending from these four indictments to further the campaign goals of the fascist movement to end our Republic.

In his 2020 book *Traitor,* David Rothkopf delivered the central historical indictment against both Donald Trump and his Constitution-destroying insurrectionist supporters in the G.O.P. And since the 2020 publication of Rothkopf's book, historical evidence to further substantiate his indictments has continued to accumulate at an ever-accelerating pace:

> [U]pon reviewing the facts, the only objective
> conclusion that can be drawn is that wittingly or
> otherwise, Donald Trump; those closest to him in
> his White House, his campaign, and his family; and
> the leaders of the Republican Party in the United
> States have committed the highest-level, greatest,
> most damaging betrayal in the history of the
> country. They are traitors. And as of this writing
> they continue to damage the United States as no
> other actors in the world can... Two and a half
> centuries after Benedict Arnold sought to ensure
> that America remained in a tyrant's grasp, Donald

In fact, as Rothkopf suggests, Trump and his supporters are guilty of a far more serious treason, since Arnold was simply working to keep the newly declared independent country under the grip of a tyrant, while Trump and his cronies, after 245 years, have been attempting to overthrow the existing Republic to install a tyranny in its place!

The argument supporting this second indictment is therefore directed to three different levels of betrayal: 1) against a G.O.P. political party supporting this tyrant's run to overthrow the Constitution; 2) against an entire political and institutional system that is not doing its job to protect and defend our constitutional system; and 3) most specifically against an ineffective justice system that is failing at every step to hold Trump accountable to the requirements of equal justice, but is instead demonstrating by every exception it grants to a man who is continually threatening prosecutors, judges, and potential witnesses against him (in ways that would have gotten any other American thrown behind bars months ago) that it is failing the most fundamental test of institutions of justice in a democratic Republic: to treat ALL citizens the same without regard to wealth, status, or political power.

As Rothkopf made clear in his 2020 book, we already had all the key information needed for history to render its verdict on the primary facts of Trump's fundamental betrayal of the American Republic, its People, and our Constitution, independent of whatever the criminal courts decide in 2024 on the specifics of his criminal conduct. Rothkopf's 2020 indictment is quite clear and concise: "The president of the U.S. is a traitor," and for historians and all students of the facts, "there is no question Trump has met every necessary standard to define his behavior as traitorous," understood as having "broken faith with the people of the country he was chosen to lead" (pp. 1-2).

And since the public historical record already provides plentiful evidence that the 45th president of the U.S. became the greatest threat this country faced during his tenure in office, how is it that the U.S. institutions that are meant to protect us, along with all the leaders who have sworn an oath to "preserve and protect" our Constitution, are allowing this traitor to run again for the highest office in the land, even after he made clear by both word and deed after 2020 that he is the sworn enemy of the very thing his oath of office swears him to serve and protect: The Constitution of the United States?!

Trump has disqualified himself many times over from being able to faithfully swear allegiance again to the presidential oath of office, so WHY are a great nation and its institutions allowing an obvious traitor to run again for election to the highest and most powerful political Office in the land? Have we and our institutions, by our complacency and lack of courage, allowed our Constitution to become a suicide pact? And does the entire leadership of the Republican party, sworn to protect and defend the Constitution, also wish to make clear its total complicity in Trump's betrayal of our Constitution? Are they all thereby willing to be complicit in the most fundamental betrayal of their oaths of office imaginable by enabling a man to seize the power to overthrow our constitutional order? It certainly seems so.

Rothkopf ironically compares Trump to our first president, who was vividly aware of how there was "scarcely any part of [his] conduct which may not hereafter be drawn into precedent," and who provided our newly constituted nation with the exemplary model of a leader who graciously stepped down from office to transfer power to the next president after him. In 1797, after serving two terms in office, president Washington thereby became the true founding exemplar of the nation's more than 220-year history of peaceful transfers of power before that history ended on January 6, 2021. For the first time in the nation's history, the 45th president of the United States, after losing the election of 2020, set a traitorous precedent by refusing to peacefully transfer power in conformity with the Constitution (*Traitor*, 42-43).

And because Trump was able to probe our nation's institutional weaknesses from within the highest office of the land, and has had extensive practice in exploiting these weaknesses from within to further aid and abet the enemies of our country, it takes little imagination to understand why handing Trump a second term in office would be even worse than the equivalent of the Germans handing Hitler the Chancellorship in 1933. As Rothkopf notes, what playwright Arthur Miller stated about the betrayal of America by antisemitic poet Ezra Pound could even more aptly be said today of Trump who held the reins of power in the highest political office in the land: "He knew all America's weaknesses and played them as expertly as Goebbels ever did" during WWII (*Traitor*, 105).

How do we protect ourselves against these continuing, ongoing attacks targeted at undermining our Constitution and national security? So far we have miserably failed to put into place the core national security protections needed to protect ourselves from the rise of a dictator intent on destroying our Republic from within. And by our failures to act creatively and decisively to defend our country, our Constitution, and our democracy, and by making it possible for Trump to be handed the reins of governmental power in 2025 just as the Germans handed power over to Hitler in 1933, we are showing ourselves to be fundamentally complicit in allowing the Trump Show to betray our country.

If we are to prevent ourselves from repeating the horrific error of German history in 1933, and step away from the path we are currently on toward handing Trump the reins of our government, let us not make the same errors in 2024 – in our second major historical opportunity to ensure that our wannabe dictator is held accountable to justice – as prosecutor Mueller did in 2019 by failing to stand up forcefully to defend our Constitution and hold Trump accountable for the crimes he has committed.

Even before the 1/6/21 insurrection, and based simply on the actual facts of the case that Mueller's investigation had uncovered, Rothkopf justly indicted the limitations of Mueller's judgments in the 2019 "Mueller Report," assessing that Mueller "was too compliant with the wishes of Trump's defenders in the G.O.P. and not robust enough in his defense of the interests of the American people, our institutions, or our Constitution":

> Each of these extraordinary, unprecedented, uncalled-for, and reckless actions [was] identical to having written the Russians a check. It is identical to having passed to the British the diagrams of the fortifications of West Point. It [was] identical to seeking to cut a deal with the British or the French or the Spanish to achieve personal gain at the expense of the country... Every betrayal has a transaction at its heart. (*Traitor*, 142-43)

The multiple "transactions" at the heart of the 2016 Trump campaign and its collusions with Russia that continued throughout the corrupt transactional presidency of Trump were clearly visible for all with eyes to see, and will constitute the most fundamental evidence for the eventual historical indictment of Trump's traitorous presidency and of all those who enabled it.

As Rothkopf argues, Trump's absurd and insurrectionist argument that "as president he had the right under Article II of the Constitution to do anything at all" constituted "a betrayal of the core ideas on which the country was founded – that no man or woman is above the law, that we are a nation of laws, and that our government is comprised of co-equal branches that provide vital checks and balances against one another" (*Traitor*, 199). And to the extent the GOP continued to support him even after it had become clear that this betrayal had become the very foundational principle of his presidency and post-presidency, this indictment of Trump's betrayal extends to every member of a sycophantic Republican Party that continues to enable Trump's ongoing insurrectionary movement to overthrow the Constitution he once swore to "preserve, protect, and defend" as president.

Furthermore, to the extent that Trump's primary goal ever since at least 2020 has been "to gain the unchecked, uncheckable power of an autocrat," with the assistance of the G.O.P. and other appointed officers of his administration, as their "Project 2025" has so clearly outlined, this alone represents, in the words of Rothkopf, "a profound betrayal by Trump, traitorous not in service of a foreign power but to ideas and principles foreign to the form of government the United States has enjoyed since our Constitution was ratified in 1789" (*Traitor*, 200).

> If you were to summarize the abuses cited in the
> articles of impeachment of Andrew Johnson,
> Richard Nixon, and Bill Clinton – for failing to follow
> federal law, failing to honor their commitments to
> preserve, protect, and defend the laws of the United
> States, for ridiculing the Congress and treating it
> with disrespect, for obstruction of justice, for abuse
> of power, and for perjury – you would find that
> Trump committed them all, often to a more
> pronounced degree than his predecessors. (204)

Many recognize the core of our national problem is not just Trump but the cultish Trumpism of the G.O.P. and 70+ million voters who were, in spite of all that was clear about Trump in 2020, still willing to vote for him. Yet, as Rothkopf concludes, "even those who recognize the dangers of this litany of crimes are proving too complacent, too inert in the face of this threat." And in the face of the complacency of all those who recognize the existential threat Trump and Trumpism represent, we now "find ourselves at one of those moments in the history of a country when there is a choice to be made, a choice between having a future and not, between… democracy and oligarchy, between what we dreamed of being and what even our founders feared we might become." And therefore "the only question that remains is, Will he be held accountable by the Congress, the courts, or now or later by the American people?" (Rothkopf 204, 222).

> This is [therefore] a moment for leaders to step up
> if we do not wish this dark moment to be a prelude
> to much worse. It is time to challenge each of these
> abuses via every legal means available… To resist
> and refuse to be complicit… [W]hatever you do,
> resist becoming numb… Everyone matters in times
> like these. Everyone must stand up for what is
> right… We are approaching a great national
> decision – in the election ahead and in the years
> that immediately follow – about whether the
> American experiment will succeed or fail, whether
> this moment does what two world wars, a civil war,
> and countless past misjudgments and missteps
> could not. We will make it together, resist, offer a
> better alternative, embrace that alternative and the
> best leaders we can find – or we will succumb, let

the inertia of some among us mark the end of what
for two and a half centuries was an idea so
compelling it inspired the world. (Rothkopf, 223)

*****

IF we are not willing to allow ourselves "to be led to the noose without protesting," and to somnambulantly embrace the dissolution of our identities, what are we to DO? How do we develop the will to ACT to end our subservience to this sickening Trump Show?

Let us not make the mistake of being like the witness in a building being set on fire by an arsonist who, instead of going after the arsonist to stop him from spreading the fire, merely runs to the window to yell for help while he allows the arsonist to continue to fuel the flames all around him. Attempting to prosecute justice while continuing to allow the criminal to commit more crimes and inflame a crowd of fellow arsonists is like this! We're all standing at the window of our burning House of Justice, yelling to onlookers that Trump must be held accountable to justice even while we are continuing to allow arsonist Trump to freely continue to support the movement of fellow arsonists in spreading the destructive fires approaching the house of our Constitution!

This is the nightmare scenario we will continue to live out so long as we are attempting to put Trump on trial while refusing to act to attack and dismantle the accelerating threat of the fascist movement that is supporting not only Trump's run for the Presidency, but his campaign to overthrow our constitutional Republic. If in the course of 2024 we seek only to prosecute Trump while doing nothing to end the Trump Show's campaign to overthrow our Constitution, we are at great risk of allowing the trials of Trump to be little more than distracting show trials while the arsonists are allowed to continue to do their destructive work of burning down the foundations of our Republic.

The most fundamental challenge facing EVERY American as well as every institutional leader of the institutions that will define how the history of 2024 plays itself out is this: Will we individually and institutionally ALLOW the Trump Show campaign for the Presidency to continue to play itself out even in face of its clear intent to overthrow our constitution? Even in the face of the clearly documented evidence of Trump's previous betrayal of the Republic, along with the 92 criminal charges for which he has now been four times indicted, what self-respecting country that values the "rule of law" would willingly provide such a traitor a clear path to taking the power needed to complete his work of destruction? Has our nation already signed its own suicide pact?

If we collectively decide to ALLOW this Trump Show to continue by doing nothing to end it in 2024, then we must all face this simple fact about how our lack of action to END the Trump Show will determine the meaning of all four trials during the course of 2024: In the context of the ongoing Trump Show, all four criminal trials may be converted by the unrestrained propaganda of the Trump Show into "show trials" for his followers, which will only further fuel a campaign strategy dedicated to overthrowing the very principles of justice these trials are meant to defend.

As we've already seen in the NY civil trial, Trump's tactics in court are just like those of Hitler in the 1924 high treason trial, where the entire focus of Hitler's effort was to cause chaos and make a mockery of the trial. Hitler played the role of star in "a grotesque circus or sensational theatrical production" that played itself out as "a masterpiece of political ignorance." As journalists of

1924 commented, the trial became a "deplorable comedy," and played itself out as a "ridiculous farce" and "parody of justice" as it became a mere platform for the broadcasting of Nazi propaganda (David King, 179, 185, 209). So the first principle of action by our House of Justice in 2024 must be: Don't allow the Trump Show to do what the Hitler Show did in 1924!

The outcome of the Hitler trial could have been different in 1924. Before the trial began, an internal Bavarian government memo revealed that the government well understood what needed to be done to effectively counter the constitutional threat posed by Hitler and his insurrection. The memo "recommended a three-pronged strategy" that included "an aggressive prosecution of the plot's ringleaders, a complete disarming of the private paramilitary bands" associated with the Nazi movement, "and a concentrated effort to discover and then block the flow of funds" that sustained the movement's organizational structure and its network of propaganda activities via newspapers and pamphlets (David King, 136).

Yet in spite of this clear vision of what needed to be done, the Bavarian and German federal governments both failed to take any of these critical steps, and thus opened German and world history to the consequences of this failure in the years to come.

Just as clearly as the Bavarian government of 1924 understood what was required to keep Hitler's movement from taking advantage of the trial to achieve its political aims, so in 2024 we can clearly see the critical three-pronged strategy that is the required foundation for any successful effort to put down the Trump Show's insurrectionary movement: 1) the aggressive prosecution of Trump and all his associated "ringleaders" of the 1/6/21 insurrection and his anti-constitutional efforts to remain in office; 2) a complete unmasking and dismantling of the core networks associated with propagating the Trumpist movement and its future insurrectionary potential; and 3) "a concentrated effort" to identify and then disrupt the flow of funds that is sustaining this fascist movement's organizational structure and network of propaganda activities.

Given these clear requirements for focusing our action, the question is: Will we and our House of Justice act to implement the core elements of such a strategy, or will we continue to allow the Trump Show to dominate our politics by failing to target our actions to shut down the Trump Show? In 2024 will the courage of our imaginative action, or our pusillanimity, determine the historical fate of our House of Justice?

*****

At bottom, the most fundamental question we must ask ourselves as we face the coming trials of 2024, is: What are the character defects of our national House of Justice (and therefore of all the citizens who constitute it) that have determined our failure so far to terminate the Trump Show? And therefore, what are the defects we all continually re-constitute by our daily failures to think and act differently than we have been? These are the defects that are setting us up to surrender our freedom as we walk like zombies to our own constitutional slaughter, and these are the defects we must therefore ruthlessly identify and address, if we wish to save our nation from destruction.

Let us therefore deeply consider the facts that support these twin indictments, and develop our supporting argument in relation to our failures of thinking and acting, in direct relation to how these failures will impact our ability to "see justice done" in the coming trials of D.J. Trump. What is the purpose of the Trump trials for the U.S. in 2024? And what will be the consequences – for the U.S. system of justice, our constitutional forms of government, and our elections, if these trials are bungled?

Indeed, will any of the substance of these trials even matter if our House of Justice surrenders its own constitutional powers of self-defense and continues to allow Trump to run for President, thereby setting the stage to allow Trump and his movement to make a mockery of these trials just as the Nazi movement did with the 1924 trial of Hitler? Hitler was found guilty of high treason, but the political muffling of the verdict rendered by his brief sentence to a country resort prison – where Hitler could work on his memoir *Mein Kampf* – fundamentally undermined what little semblance of "justice" was rendered by that verdict. Such a ludicrous verdict and sentence, on top of the propaganda coup for the insurrectionists achieved by the trial itself, guaranteed that the outcome of the trial would feed the political campaigning needs and power of Hitler's fascist movement.

THE fundamental challenge of 2024 for the American people and its institutions of both justice and law-regulated government therefore concerns whether the Trump Show campaign will be allowed to continue in the face of these trials. If the Trump Show is allowed to continue unobstructed, all of the trials will be at risk of being manipulated into political show trials by the constant barrage of propaganda produced by the Trump Show, in spite of the best efforts of prosecutors and Judges to prevent this.

Due to an almost incomprehensible weakness in our constitutional structure and system of election laws, which fails to automatically ban indicted criminals from running for the highest political offices of the land, we will all stand witness to whether justice is seen to be done to a twice impeached and four-times criminally indicted former President who has so far been treated as if he is truly above the law, to the fundamental betrayal of the principles of American constitutional democracy and justice.

III.

Judgments Issued
to the U.S. House of Justice

Lying is the message. It's not just that both Putin and Trump lie, it is that they lie in the same way and for the same purpose: blatantly, ***to assert power over truth itself.*** Take, for example, Putin's statements on Ukraine. In March 2014 he claimed that there were no Russian troops in newly annexed Crimea; a month later he affirmed that Russians troops had been on the ground. Throughout 2014 and 2015, he repeatedly denied that Russian troops were fighting in eastern Ukraine; in 2016 he easily acknowledged that they were there. In each case, Putin insisted on lying in the face of clear and convincing evidence to the contrary, and in each case his subsequent shift to truthful statements were not admissions given under duress: they were proud, even boastful affirmatives made at his convenience. Together, they communicated a single message: Putin's power lies in being able to say what he wants, when he wants, regardless of the facts. He is president of his country and king of reality. *(Masha Gessen, NY Review of Books, 12.13.2016)*

III. Judgments Issued to the U.S. House of Justice

> Our only hope for learning and changing ... is to confront the past as it was, without defense mechanisms, but with an understanding that the future is still open for change," and has available to it a stabilizing force of judgment which can provide "the starting point from which to change, to begin something new. (Hannah Arendt, "Truth and Politics," *Between Past and Future*, 1968)

Judgment 1.

If we engage the imaginative thinking required – as the existential foundation of true democratic Action – to develop an effective plan of action for disempowering the Trump Show in the course of 2024, then it will be possible for the U.S. House of Justice to show justice being done to Trump and Trumpism, and "we the people" will be successful in doing our duty to support and defend the Constitution from those seeking to destroy it.

But if we fail to make this imaginative political turn, then we will all stand by as political spectators in 2024 and watch helplessly while we allow our institutions of justice to collapse in their efforts to defend our Constitution, and we will all subsequently witness our constitutional republic dissolve before our eyes, as did the people of Germany in the months after January 1933 when Hitler was handed the reins of the Chancellorship by political leaders who thought they could control him.

Judgment 2.

If we engage the decisive action that the disqualification clause of the 14th Amendment of our Constitution calls for, and in regard to the trials of Trump support and fight for our Constitution and thereby refuse to continue to allow it to be abused and made a mockery of by the Trump Show; if we take justice back and become its heroic champions at every level of our constitutional democracy – from local school boards and election offices, to state and federal political offices – by demanding that both we the people and our institutions of justice live up to the ideals of justice and democratic citizenship embodied in our Constitution and the struggles of our history; If we thereby work to rebuild the strength of our democratic institutions, then we will save our country from continuing to slide down the slope of political anarchy into a constitutional apocalypse.

But if we fail to take this turn into decisive action during 2024, and fail to take up the power and responsibility of our role as citizens to defend our Constitution and our democracy, then we will be forced to watch as the Trump show makes a mockery of our Constitution and will become, through our inaction, effective colluders with the Trump Show in the destruction of our Republic, even before the 2024 elections occur. And in the face of such failure of political vision and will, we will fall like zombies into line into another terrible historical "procession of human beings marching like dummies to their deaths" as we mechanically watch the historical calendar turn from 2024 to 2025.

And then, indeed, the entire world will once again stand witness to the horrible spectacle of seeing an entire nation of people surrender to the triumph of totalitarian fascism by renouncing and abandoning their citizenship "to the point of ceasing to affirm their own democratic political identity."

People of the United States, let this NOT be the history we write for ourselves during 2024!

Verdict rendered to citizen Trump:

"And if it is true that 'justice must not only be done but must be seen to be done,'" as Arendt emphasized (*Eichmann in Jerusalem*, 277), then it must be stressed *now* that the justice of what MUST be done in the trials of 2024 will only emerge *to be seen by all* IF the judges presiding over each of the trials of D.J. Trump dare to address their defendant in something like the following terms:

"Donald J. Trump, in spite of whatever claims you make to being innocent of the charges rendered against you by this Court – in defiance of the actual facts of the case which have been placed so clearly in evidence before us during this trial, and which you seek to deny in your alternative propaganda universe of lies that continually testify to the fundamental ways in which you betray every principle of justice and truth on which human community and solidarity are based – and based on the actual facts of evidence before us, which you clearly wish you had the absolute power to erase from existence, but which this court, in its faithful dedication to the mission of preserving and defending the U.S. Constitution, will not grant you the absolute power to accomplish, this abundant evidence testifies loudly and clearly to the fact that you have carried out, and therefore actively supported, a policy of mass fraud and obstruction of justice, thereby violating your most fundamental obligations to protect and defend the people and Constitution of the United States.

For as Hannah Arendt noted in her judgment on Adolf Eichmann, "politics is not like the nursery; in politics obedience and support are the same." And just as you supported and carried out, while seeking to compel obedience to, a policy of mass fraud against the people of the United States, and against their rights to vote in free and fair elections – as though you and your subordinates had any right to determine who should and who should not have the right to vote – we find that no American can be expected to want to share with you the right to continue to make decisions about their rights. This is the reason you must be found guilty, and held accountable for the gravest offense that any political leader of a democratic Republic can commit: the offence of betraying your own most basic duties and responsibilities of presidential office to "protect and defend the Constitution of the United States against all enemies foreign and domestic."

Rather than defending the Constitution, your brazen and continuing lies and politics of fraud have turned you into our Constitution's sworn enemy, and therefore this Court, in defense of that Constitution you have so deeply betrayed, now decisively and unequivocally declares you to be guilty as charged. And on behalf of all the people of the United States who have been so egregiously wronged by your campaign of fraud against them and our Constitution, this Court now adjudicates your just sentence to be, at minimum, the loss of any future right to ever represent the people of the United States again in any office of this land, as long as you shall continue to live, and will seek to ensure all other criminal penalties are rendered against you according to the principle you so completely betrayed: Equal justice for all.

Epilogue

A Call to Action: "ENOUGH!"

Criminal proceedings...rest on laws whose 'essence' ... is that a crime is not committed only against the victim but primarily against the community whose law is violated. The wrongdoer is brought to justice because his act has disturbed and gravely endangered the community as a whole, and not because, as in civil suits, damage has been done to individuals who are entitled to reparation. The reparation effected in criminal cases is of an altogether different nature; it is the body politic itself that stands in need of being 'repaired,' and it is the general public order that has been thrown out of gear and must be restored, as it were. It is, in other words, the law, not the plaintiff, that must prevail. (Hannah Arendt, *Eichmann in Jerusalem*, 1963).

Epilogue

So let it be clear that the core indictments leveled here against the U.S. "House of Justice" amount to this:

By ALLOWING a four-time indicted criminal, who has publicly declared in both word and deed his intent to overthrow our Constitution, to run again for our highest government office, we the people have so far failed to fulfill our duties "to support and defend the Constitution of the United States against all enemies, foreign and domestic." And it is due to our twinned failures to think imaginatively and act decisively to put an end to this Trump Show that we are allowing ourselves to continue to be "tortured victims" of a zombie-like march to our own political apocalypse.

Therefore our chief duty NOW – if we want to fulfill our responsibilities to support and defend the Constitution of the United States against all enemies – is to correct our failures to act decisively since 2021 by *awakening our imaginations* to the potential we have *now* to *act decisively to terminate* the horrors of the

Trump Show that will otherwise lead us to far worse horrors.

If we bow down to the power of the Trump Show by allowing it to continue to dominate our political life throughout 2024, we will be condemning ourselves and our constitutional mode of democratic self-government to destruction. We must come to fully recognize and understand that the totalitarian threat of the forces of Injustice we are facing will not be stopped in their campaign to destroy all we value except by the full and lucid application of the countervailing forces of Law and Justice. If we continue to fail to fight strategically for the victory of truth and justice over the lies and totalitarian violence being propagated by Trump and the fascist political movement embraced and enabled by the former "Republican" Party, we will be submitting ourselves to destruction as surely as the German people did in 1932-33 by allowing their political divisions and confusion to pave the way for placing the reins of governmental power into the hands of Hitler on January 30, 1933.

In the trials ahead we are either fully committed to the action required of us to fight for justice to end the Trump Show, in defense of our Constitution, or by our inaction we will allow justice to be betrayed into the violent manipulative arms of the fascist propaganda movement that seeks to convert all of Trump's criminal trials into political show trials that further the "Trump Show" campaign of Injustice. Whether the Trump criminal trials descend into farcical show trials will depend on whether we continue to allow the Trump Show to dictate their political meaning by failing to attack and shut down the power of the Trump Show's instruments of propaganda and political manipulation. Our success or failure to shut down the Trump Show's power in 2024 will determine not only the historical outcome of these trials, but the impact these trials exert on the November elections that will determine the fate of our nation and the world in the years ahead.

*****

In conclusion, let us turn back once more to the testimony offered by one man who experienced and attempted to communicate the horror that results from a nation's failure to act in the face of the dramaturgy of the politics of fascism and its cult of absolute power, which Donald J. Trump and his Party of sycophants is furthering in our own day:

> The triumph of [of totalitarian fascism] demands that the tortured victim allow himself to be led to the noose without protesting, that he renounce and abandon himself to the point of ceasing to affirm his identity. And [this] is not for nothing… They know that the system which succeeds in destroying its victim before he mounts the scaffold…is incomparably the best for keeping a whole people in slavery. In submission. Nothing is more terrible than these processions of human beings going like dummies to their deaths. (David Rousset, Buchenwald inmate, *Les Jours de notre mort*, 1947)

In the political outcomes of the 2024 trials of Trump, the entire American nation is the potential victim, since the Trump Show is demanding that we the people betray our own identity by colluding with its campaign for a presidency that will be dedicated to overthrowing the very Constitution the presidency is pledged to defend. Due to our political failures to act decisively in 2021 to 2023, we've allowed Trump to successfully mount his third campaign for the presidency, even after he so clearly betrayed everything our Constitution and the nation's historical struggles for justice and equality have stood for!

And still in 2024 we are being told by many of our leaders and political pundits that the best our institutions can do to defend us from this fate is to collude with Trump in allowing him to run again for the Presidency even in the face of his complete betrayal. We are being asked to allow our nation to be "led to the noose without protesting, to renounce our identities as citizens of a constitutional Republic – and to surrender that Republic into the hands of those producers of the Trump Show who have clearly announced their intent to destroy it. In other words, we are being asked to allow our nation to become the willing victim of this Trump Show, and to submit our nation to its own destruction even before the elections of 2024 occur. Nothing indeed is more terrible than a procession of human beings, let alone an entire nation of human beings, willing to "go like dummies to their deaths!"

It is our duty, as citizens, not to allow our thinking, our imagination, or our actions to be defined by this narrow understanding of our non-choices as we walk forward into the history of 2024. We can think and act otherwise than this kind of non-thinking seeks to limit us to. And *we must think and act differently,* if we wish to act as citizens to save ourselves, our Constitution, and our democracy from the fate that the Trump Show wants all of us to submit to, as we pave the way for this new form of totalitarianism to seize power over our country without a fight.

So, again, the most fundamental question now facing the U.S. "House of Justice" is this:

Are "we the People" of the United States truly going to allow ourselves to be hung by the noose of Trumpism without a fight? Will we willingly and deliberately surrender our existence as a democratic Republic to our own destroyer? This is precisely what appears to be happening, as a sleepwalking nation allows a proven tyrant who has sworn himself to the destruction of the constitutional republic to run for the highest office of the land for a third time, as if the nation with all the power of its institutions is paralyzed to do anything about it! So if you think such an abject surrender is absolutely disgusting to contemplate, it's now time to demand of yourselves and your leaders that we do something about it!

*****

Trump and his enablers are now seeking from our U.S. House of Justice – through the guise of the Trump Show's 2024 presidential campaign – the permission structure to overthrow our Constitution and install a totalitarian dictatorship in 2025. This means that the clear existential question facing all of us who live within the U.S. House of Justice in 2024 is: Will we hand Trump what he wants, as the Germans did for Hitler in January 1933, or will we act decisively in 2024 to shut the Trump Show down and commit it to the bin of historical horrors where it belongs?

In the Epilogue to her book Enough (2023), Cassidy Hutchinson summarizes how she had "resisted being a part of efforts to hold [Trump] accountable for his actions." But after the January 6 insurrection she realized she wanted the truth to be known, "had seen how fragile democracy is, and [her] conscience recognized our duty as citizens to attend to it for its survival." And so she "changed course, choosing to follow through on the promise I made when I swore the oath to protect and defend the United States" (Hutchinson, 354-355). And as a result of this decision to change course, in her courageous 2022 testimony before the House January 6th Committee she effectively declared to the world and to the criminal betrayals of the Trump Show, "Enough!"

2024 presents the opportunity for all of us as a people and a nation to follow the examples of courageous citizens like E. Jean Carroll and Cassidy Hutchinson to wake up, change course, and choose to ACT on the promises we all make when we "pledge allegiance to the flag of the United States and the Constitution for which it stands, one nation, under God, indivisible, with liberty and justice for all."

For every time we and our leaders allow Trump to get away with threatening prosecutors, judges and witnesses, without treating him just like any other American would be treated by throwing him behind bars: We are walking like dummies to the noose of our own political destruction...

Every time we and our leaders allow Trump's followers to threaten those he targets in his social media posts and rallies, and do nothing to hold Trump and his followers accountable for these threats of violence: We are walking like dummies to the noose...

Every time judges and our courts of law allow Trump to be treated differently than all other Americans, to be treated as if he is special, just because he was a former president (and is wealthy and perceived to be powerful) – instead of being treated as someone equal to all Americans before the law – we are walking like dummies to the noose...

Every time judges and prosecutors allow Trump to get away with things no other American under criminal indictment would be allowed to get away with, we are walking like dummies to the noose of our own political destruction!

So let us all now awake from our unthinking complicity with the Trump Show and its fascist movement toward the dismantling and destruction of our constitution and nation. Let us all now rise up together to shout "Enough!" with thunder, and summon the power of our individual and collective imaginations to create ways to ACT TOGETHER to END the Trump Show and our zombie-like procession in sync with it, which can only lead to our national apocalypse. Let us all, in other words, stop marching like dummies to the noose of our own political destruction!

ENOUGH!

The general Government . . . can never be in danger of degenerating into a monarchy, an Oligarchy, an Aristocracy ... so long as there shall remain any virtue in the body of the People. (President George Washington)

The ***transcendence of revelation*** lies precisely in the fact that the epiphany comes, in the Saying, from the one who receives the revelation... The Infinite thus has glory only through subjectivity, [but not the subjectivity of the 'inner adventure' of a self-contained soul, **but]** ***through the human adventure of the approach of the other***. (Emmanuel Levinas, "Truth of Disclosure and Truth of Testimony," 1972)

Renewal becomes impossible if one supposes things to be constant that are not – safety, for example, or money, or power. One clings then to chimeras, by which one can only be betrayed, and the entire hope – the entire possibility – of freedom disappears. ***And by destruction I mean precisely the abdication by Americans of any effort really to be free.*** (James Baldwin, *The Fire Next Time*, 1963)

Forthcoming (May, 2024), from
Undoing the Folded Lie of Trumpism:

A Political Strategy for
Crushing the Fascist Beast of Trumpism
[Excerpts]

And the more heavily the scales are weighted in favor of disaster, the more miraculous will the deed done in freedom appear; for it is disaster, not salvation, which always happens automatically and therefore always must appear to be irresistible. Objectively, that is, seen from the outside and without taking into account that man is a beginning and a beginner, the chances that tomorrow will be like yesterday are always overwhelming... (Arendt, *Between Past and Future*, 169)

A Political Strategy for Crushing the Fascist Beast of Trumpism

What We are Fighting Against

In summary, what is Trumpism? What are we fighting against?

1) Trumpism is *the abdication of Thinking*, the surrender of thinking to a *politics of lies* dictated by the Fuhrer and his Trumpist cult, and dedicated to the overthrow of truth itself.

2) Based on the overthrow of truth and all institutions of truth-telling, Trumpism *abdicates all responsibility for ethical judgment and action*, and thereby **seeks to overthrow all personal responsibility for our shared human community, and for the preservation of human life itself.** This complete abdication of responsibility for human life has already been exhibited most horribly not only by Trump's intentionally weak response to the Covid-19 pandemic, which resulted in the *deaths of over half a million Americans in 2020.* This intentional abdication

of responsibility was also manifested by the cruelty and arbitrary, irresponsible decision-making of Trump's border policy – which included the separation of families and the infamous detention centers for immigrant children – and his withdrawal from the Paris Accord on Climate Change, which abdicated our nation's responsibility for working with the rest of the world to prevent the potential civilization-destroying impact of unmitigated climate change over the coming century.

3) Trumpism is the *abdication of constitutional democratic politics* in pursuit of a totalitarian will to power →

Trumpism is therefore a fascist totalitarian movement dedicated to the overthrow of our constitutional Republic. THIS is what we are fighting. *There can be no effective resistance to* Trumpism *that does not completely comprehend and grapple with THIS reality. There can be no effective political movement to counter Trumpism that does not develop a clear strategy* *to defeat it based on both an understanding of what we are fighting against,* **and** *what we are fighting for.*

And so, having defined what we are fighting against, we must now turn toward the task of understanding how we find the resources to wage this fight, and to understand more clearly what exactly we are *fighting for*, and what we must do to wage that fight courageously and effectively.

> Be primitive in action;
> a strategist, in foresight.
>
> —René Char
> *Feuillets d'Hypnos*

What We Must Do *Together* to Crush the Fascist Beast of *Trumpism*

In every era the attempt must be made anew to wrest tradition away from a conformism that is about to overpower it. The Messiah comes not only as the redeemer, he comes as the *subduer of Antichrist.* (Walter Benjamin)

To become sober is: to come so close to oneself in one's understanding, one's knowing, that all one's understanding becomes ACTION. (Kierkegaard, *Judge For Yourselves!,* 130)

And if you *fail to act,* hiding from yourself and from others behind a screen of deliberation, you bring down the responsibility solely upon yourself *as an individual…* Purity of heart is to will one thing (Kierkegaard, *Purity of Heart,* 189)

Our Existential Political Crisis

When faced with the existential challenge of the dissolution of our Republic by the *fascist threat of Trumpism,* there can be no hesitation about the need for *immediate action,* together with others, to actively RISE and join the FIGHT to defeat this threat. The growing evil of non-thinking knaves and fools, who are attempting to take over our politics and destroy our democratic experiment in freedom – our legacy of struggle to create a more perfect union – cannot be tolerated if we wish to "keep" this Republic.

For *if* WE don't learn to *stand up* for our democratic freedoms through engaging an effective and courageous *strategy of resistance* to this fascist movement, and *act to renew* the institutions of our free Republic, then those who are acting politically to destroy our democratic republic will win. No one will step in from outside to save us from our own *inaction* in the face of the ultimate *banality of evil* that Trumpism is! In fact, our nation's enemies, like Putin's Russia, are actively working from the outside to strengthen the power of this *banality of evil* to destroy the United States from within, without ever having to fire a shot. ***Trumpism* is the ultimate *Trojan horse* of U.S. democracy.**

We fall silent in dumbfounded perplexity in response to the sheer unprecedented absurdity of the politics of Trumpism's *Big Lie* – because we find it so hard to take seriously, to give it credence, to understand its power, or to believe it has the power to define reality for so many millions of our fellow Americans – even as we watch in stunned amazement as it mobilizes tens of millions on its behalf, and see tens of millions of our fellow citizens consent to bowing down to its absurdities, turning over their money to its cause, and sacrificing their wills and votes in devotion to it. How do we confront and counter the confounding force of the *banality of evil* represented by *Trumpism*, as embodied in the sycophantic consent of the GOP to the speech and actions of 1/6/21 and its aftermath, not to mention the willingness of the GOP in 2024 to support a two-times impeached and four-times criminally indicted corrupt man to run for President again?

As this essay has argued, the core barriers to engaging an *effective Resistance* are the lack of clear comprehension of the nature of the political movement we are fighting against, our failures to confront and overcome the cowardice and banality of evil in ourselves, and the lack of a clear political vision and strategy for defeating the fascist totalitarian movement of *Trumpism*. Fascism feeds on the weakness and sources of corruption in all of us. And just as a bully will continue to grow in strength until someone stands up *firmly* against him to swat the bully down, so a fascist movement will continue to grow until a united political force stands up to the political bully and says – *with the organized power of a nation united to back these words up by ACTION –* "ENOUGH! NO MORE!"

The *fascist* threat that Trumpism represents will not go away until enough of us take up the responsibility of our democratic powers as citizens, and take ACTION in solidarity with others to STAND UP to the bully movement of Trumpism to say to both the movement and its petty fuhrers through our organized political action, "NO MORE!" We will do this by standing up and *acting together* against the automatism of the non-thinking crowd of sycophants working to destroy the foundations of our constitutional democracy and the institutions of our common *political community*.

So the central question facing us now is this: **HOW do we accomplish the *strategic goal* of mobilizing, *in short order*, a united political movement capable of rising to the challenge of stopping and *crushing* this fascist bully movement of Trumpism,** which is now working to seize the reins of government power so it can turn these powers against "we the people" and destroy our democratic republic?

We now need a clear strategic vision for *how* we will work together *throughout 2024* to summon both the *courage* and the *will* to 1) RAISE UP a *true resistance movement* of democratic solidarity to fight FOR the treasures of our democratic citizenship and 2) CRUSH the ongoing insurgency of the fascist beast in our midst!

The totalitarian beast of *Trumpism* is feeding on the weakness and sources of corruption and disunity in all of us! Therefore, if we want to crush it, we must take both individual and collective responsibility for addressing these common sources of our weakness, so we can raise out of the ashes of our common failures the organized democratic power needed to counter the core source of fascism's corrupting force: its ability to prey on our collective weakness and divisions against each other.

Once we have developed effective political mechanisms for countering that core mechanism of corruption, we will have gained the power to cut the beast off from its food sources (of money and propaganda), and THAT is our common strategic goal: to starve the beastly body of *Trumpism* into a weakness that allows us to attack and crush its head, its political source, so it can no longer continue to lay waste to our institutions of political community and common humanity.

Since this beast draws its power from consuming and degrading the institutional sources of our political community, the minute we join together in an effective resistance movement to defend these institutional sources and strengthen their bulwarks against the continuing depredations of this beast, *from that moment we will begin cut the beast off from its food sources and begin starving it into defeat.* None of us can do this alone. We need to act in solidarity with each other as the common political party of democratic humanity standing against the beast that seeks to destroy everything we value together as the foundation of our common, but fragile, human world. *And **unless** we act together now to starve and crush this beast, we will all watch helplessly together as this beast destroys our common democratic world, as it did in Europe during the 1930s.*

This time the fascist beast is raising its fiendish head here in the United States. So it is up to us, *the people of these United States*, to cut off the beast's head to ensure the 2020s in the United States do not follow the path of Germany in the 1930s, when the Nazis were *allowed by*

Germany's leaders and citizens to seize power in 1933, and then quickly convert the German democratic state into a fascist one-party totalitarian dictatorship.

*****

Toward a Political Strategy of Resistance built on the *Treasures* of Our Democratic Citizenship

Part One of this essay analyzed WHAT we are fighting against, to provide a clear sense of the specific elements of the fascist totalitarian movement we are committed to resisting. As summarized above:

1) Trumpism is the **abdication of Thinking**, the surrender of thinking to a politics of lies dictated by the Fuhrer and his Trumpist cult, and dedicated to the overthrow of truth itself.

2) Based on the overthrow of truth and all institutions of truth-telling, Trumpism abdicates all responsibility for ethical judgment and action, and thereby ***seeks to overthrow all personal responsibility for our shared human community***, and for the preservation of human life itself.

3) Trumpism is the abdication of constitutional democratic politics in pursuit of a totalitarian will to power → **Trumpism is therefore a fascist totalitarian movement dedicated to the overthrow of our constitutional Republic.**

THIS is what we are fighting. *There can be no effective resistance to* Trumpism *that does not completely comprehend and grapple with THIS reality.* And, there can be no effective political movement to counter *Trumpism* that does not develop a clear strategy to defeat it based on both an understanding of what we are fighting against, *and* what we are *fighting for.*

To mount an effective resistance movement, as this entire book has emphasized, it is not enough to know only what we are fighting against. As *Part Two* emphasized, we must also clearly understand and *take responsibility for* what it is we're fighting *for*: the treasures of our democratic citizenship. It's an understanding of this spiritual "home territory" we're defending that creates the foundation for the most impassioned and effective resistance. For if *Trumpism* is the abdication of human responsibility for ethical judgment and action, and works to overthrow all personal ethical responsibility for our shared human community and the preservation of human life, we must powerfully and clearly RECLAIM that responsibility and fight for it, as the foundation of our resistance movement. *Together we reclaim our responsibility for this fight by developing an effective strategy and uniting around that strategy to crush the fascist beast in our midst.*

So let us now turn to a full and direct focus on the third component of understanding what *true resistance* means: the *political strategy* of resistance built on the foundation of the treasures of democracy and the inspired soul of democratic citizenship. For *here* is the ground on which we stand to prosecute our fight against the fascist beast. And unless we all come together in a common understanding and organized strategy for renewing not just the *political spirit* of democracy, but also its *political agency and power* – through the dedicated work of citizenship that is required to rebuild and strengthen the soul of our democratic INSTITUTIONS – we will be trying to fight the fascist enemy with our hands tied behind our backs while standing in quicksand.

Failure to achieve a clear understanding of our common mission and strategy to defend and strengthen our core institutions of democratic truth-telling is our political quicksand. And if we don't build a clear bridge over that quicksand, we will allow the fascist movement to take possession of, and destroy our democratic treasures. At that moment our democratic institutions collapse and our great democratic experiment collapses with them. And *that* collapse will constitute the ignominious end of the story of America's great "experiment" in democracy brought about by the MAGA non-thinking of the Trumpist mob.

So what are the core components of an *effective political strategy of resistance* to crush the fascist beast of Trumpism?:

1) **Establish the Foundation**: Develop a new democratic political movement to defend and strengthen our core institutions of democratic citizenship: education, the news media, and our system of justice (courts, judicial appointments, systems of judicial nomination and election).

2) **Take the Offensive** against the core elements of fascist movement-building (its processes of development), including its central propaganda outlets and funding sources, which feed the fascist beast: "The best defense is an aggressive offense" – Attack and cut off the primary sources of fuel

sustaining and growing the Trumpist movement: it's corrupt funding sources & propaganda outlets.

3) **Defend Democracy** – Work the strategy to:

a) STOP and counter the work of the fascist beast to overthrow the electoral institutions that guarantee fair elections by doing all that is necessary to shame the U.S. Senate into ACTION to PASS strong Voting Rights legislation that will reverse the ongoing efforts of the fascist GOP to rig the 2024 elections in ways that facilitate their seizure of power.

b) STOP the fascist brownshirt tactics of violent threat, intimidation, and action by demanding that our justice systems aggressively pursue, arrest, and hold the perpetrators of these violent tactics accountable for their crimes.

These three components of an effective resistance strategy are intimately interconnected since the development of each one depends on the work of the other components. There can be no effective work to counter any of the core components of fascist movement without a strong movement of democratic citizenship (component 1) that provides the positive foundation for the work to starve and crush the fascist beast (components 2 and 3). And there can be no effective work to counter the GOP efforts of voter suppression (component 3) unless components 1 and 2 are developing apace.

1. Establish the Foundation:
Build a Vibrant Political Counter-Movement to Take "Responsibility" for Our Democracy

To establish the proper foundation for our resistance, we must develop a new democratic political movement to defend and strengthen our *core institutions* of *democratic citizenship*: education, the news media, and our systems of justice – our courts, judicial appointments, systems of judicial nomination and election, etc.

As *Part Two* exposed, the degrading *processes* of fascism are able to take over our institutions of political power, one after the other, only so long as we, as individuals, *surrender* the sources of power we have through our own connections to democratic institutions and our fellow citizens – our common bonds of citizenship. This surrender occurs as we *allow* our common political bonds to be weakened and dissolved through corrupting attractions to the lowest common denominators of lust, greed, hatred/resentment, and will to power. And it is the primary goal of fascist propaganda efforts to broadcast and empower these seductive attractions, as that propaganda channel masquerading as *FOX NEWS* has so clearly demonstrated.

As *Part Two* of this book also elaborated, in circumstances where "political life has become petrified and political action [has become] impotent to interrupt [these] automatic *processes [of decay]*... freedom is not experienced as a mode of being with its own kind of 'virtue' and 'virtuosity,' but as a supreme gift" of the isolated few/elite. And so no wonder the masses turn against such an elitist "freedom" of the few in a resentment that further fuels the fires of fascist populism. In such a context, these *automatic processes* of political decay "can only spell ruin to human life" (Arendt, *Between Past and Future*, 167).

But, as Arendt also observes, "what usually remains intact [even] in the epochs of petrification and foreordained doom is the *faculty of freedom itself*, the *sheer capacity to begin, which animates and inspires all human activities and is the hidden source of production of all great and beautiful things*. But so long as this source remains hidden" from public view, and alienated from the public participation of the people in the kind of public happiness of solidarity our political founders experienced, freedom remains unpolitical like an unworldly disembodied ghost isolated from the reality of politics. The *re-worlding* of freedom is instantiated through a rebirth of public engagement with, and struggles to strengthen, our core democratic institutions of education, public media/the press, and our institutions of justice.

It is in the *moment when freedom steps forth decisively and courageously into the public realm*, and takes its place of responsibility as part of a united cause freely accessible to all who want to participate in public *action*, that the miracle previewed in *Part Two* steps into history: the *appearance* of the inevitable necessity or doom of events is shattered by the advent of a *new beginning* of political action. This new beginning of political action stands up to, and goes to battle with, the violent automatism of historical inevitability, *to call its bluff!*

And this bluff is called precisely when an aroused citizenry takes up the work of defending and strengthening our institutions of truth-telling to secure them from degrading depredation and overthrow by the politics of lies. *This* is when *public freedom* is born anew, and public happiness or solidarity is rediscovered through the *instauration* of a new politics of *action* to renew the institutions of truth-telling that forge the bonds of citizenship in the present with the tradition of past struggles to *free all* from slavery to tyranny, greed, and the will of some to assert unlimited power over others.

The treasures we uncover in that moment of awakening and recommitment to the public freedom of democratic institution-building are the treasures of our true democratic citizenship, which provide the key to the forms of political action in concert with others needed to mount an *effective resistance against fascism* to prevent it from winning and destroying all we hold dear. These treasures of our democratic citizenship give us the resources needed not only to deconstruct the mechanisms of growth that allow fascist totalitarian movements to develop and seize power. These treasures also give us resources needed to champion a powerful new activism of democratic truth-telling that becomes the pulsing heart of a *rebirth of democratic institutions.* And it is this rebirth of democratic institutions that provides the most potent vaccine to the *political virus of Trumpism* that is currently corrupting our core institutions of news, education, and justice to *destroy democracy* rather than strengthen it.

2. Take the Offensive: "The best defense is an effective offense"

Since the project of renewing our democratic institutions of truth-telling is intimately intertwined with the project of countering the propaganda of lies that is the tip of the fascist movement's sword for destroying our institutions, we can't discuss the work of democratic institution-building without first taking into consideration what is needed to fight and counter the politics of lies that is the foundation of fascism. For the process of renewing our democratic institutions of truth-telling will grow out of our work of taking the offensive against the core elements of fascist movement-building, beginning with the virus-like spread of its destructive propaganda of lies.

Indeed, "taking the offensive" against fascism means taking our fight to the home territory of the fascist movement's core elements and processes of development. If the best defense of democracy is an effective and aggressive offense against its enemies, then *we must direct our attack toward cutting off the primary sources of fuel sustaining and growing the Trumpist movement: it's propaganda outlets, and its corrupt funding sources.*

*****

***Thinking in Action*:**
Countering the Politics of the *Big Lie* and its Abdication of Thinking

Strategy #1: Since propaganda efforts to promote *the Big Lie* are the originating and energizing core of the fascist movement's efforts to build up an alternate universe of political reality based on the easy manipulability of the Fuhrer's lies – which can then be used to displace and war against the common world of facts that is the stabilizing]foundation of the established democratic political order – the **first and primary task of any defense and renewal of democratic institutions** is to develop a clear strategy for *attacking and undermining the propaganda outlets and networks of the fascist movement.*

An effective anti-propaganda strategy will have two main objectives that counter the two primary objectives of the fascist propaganda effort: First, since fascist propaganda and its corrupt apostles are dedicated to converting individuals over to a shared faith in the *Big Lie* by convincing people to surrender the responsibility of thinking and judging for themselves in order to give their minds and souls over to forms of semi-religious indoctrination detached from independent thinking, our counter-strategy must be precisely and implacably directed at *unmasking and revealing the methods and sources of these fascist indoctrination efforts.* Just as fascist propaganda attacks reasoned thinking, grounded in evidence and facticity, so our counter-propaganda strategy is based in an implacable insistence on developing resources throughout our culture that strengthen our ties to rational fact-based thinking in all aspects of education, the news media, and institutions of justice.

Strategy #2: Since fascist propaganda is dedicated to undermining our attachment to the institutions that sustain our common shared world of facticity by constant militant assaults on our core truth-telling institutions of justice, education, and the news media – to deprive these institutions of their ability to be the bulwark that sustains the established norms of a democratic political order – our second strategy of resistance is dedicated to the *constant strengthening of popular understanding and attachment to these institutions* that are the core of our democratic existence.

Countering the Violent "Bully Politics" of Domination

Strategy #3: Our third strategy of resistance develops tactical methods for countering and attacking the four core elements of fascist propaganda's "bully politics" of domination:

1) While fascist propaganda pukes contempt for all established forms of intellectual and organized, rational

debate – with the objective of overthrowing truth itself – our resistance strategy constantly defends and promotes the fundamental values of intellectual and reasoned discourse and debate;

2) While fascist propaganda rejects all forms of shared agreement to abide by the standards of reasoned political compromise and debate, since these are the very structures of democracy that allow politics to be governed by the peaceful battle of ideas grounded in shared consent to the rule of truth and facts, our resistance strategy is dedicated to the *creative, constant defense and promotion of a shared commitment to the standards of reasoned political debate, based on evidentiary facts and norms of truth-telling* that are the foundation of a nonviolent democratic political order. Our strategy will strongly and clearly establish such agreement to common standards of truth-telling as the *necessary foundation* for any engagement in political debate.

This means that individuals and parties that make clear their unwillingness to abide by such reasonable standards of engagement will ***forfeit their right*** to be included in the official political forums of election debate, for the same reasons that we reject negotiations with terrorists. And fascism is, after all, in its rejection of all standards of truth for purposes of reasoned compromise, a form of political terrorism grounded root and branch in violence. Just as we do not negotiate with terrorists, neither does any self-respecting democratic political order allow bullies to determine the rules of political debate. Anyone unwilling to be judged by, and abide by, the rules of evidence and argument based on facts *disqualifies* themselves from the realm of political debate and consideration for democratic election. *These political norms of reasoned debate must be strengthened and enforced if any democratic political order is to survive.*

3) While fascist propaganda declares war on all established forms of social and political order, including the rule of law, as it works to blow up the established norms and institutions grounded in common consent to the rule of truth and law, our strategy of resistance *champions the rule of truth and law as the basis of all civilized and democratic political order.* This does not mean our strategy of resistance is uncritical of existing

norms and institutions, but it clearly recognizes that all constructive critique of existing institutions must be grounded in a common commitment to the rule of truth and law.

4) And finally, while fascist propaganda is grounded in a clear willingness to give consent to the violent action that is the culmination of its "any means necessary" strategy for accomplishing its overthrow of the established political order, our strategy of resistance is planted firmly on a commitment to opposing and holding accountable to the rule of law ALL who would use violence and threats of violence as a means to achieving their political objectives. And in the service of this strategy, our resistance movement is devoted to strengthening the laws and resources of the *institutions of justice* responsible for pursuing and prosecuting the violent extremists in our midst, along with their promoters and facilitators.

Countering the Politics of Division & Disunification

Strategy #4: Finally, because the deepest emotional components of the logic of fascist propaganda and its movement are those dedicated to using all existing anxieties over group differences to drive a wedge between groups as the most fundamental tactic of its strategy to divide and conquer a democratic nation – by constantly pitting groups against each other – our *fourth strategy of resistance is firmly committed to the hard work of building bridges of mutual understanding and collaboration across lines of difference as the most foundational labor of a strongly diverse, multicultural politics of political resistance.* For just as surely as fascist movements recognize their greatest enemy is the diverse force of coalitions united together against the fascist movement, so our strategy of resistance makes the building and strengthening of such diverse coalitions a primary foundation of our fight against the propaganda and political tactics of fascism.

Instead of allowing the fascist movement and its propaganda to exploit differences of race, religion, gender, sexuality, economic class, and political ideology to its recruiting advantage, our resistance strategy recognizes the diversity of perspectives represented within our country as one of the great resources that nurtures our democracy so long as we work constantly to embrace these differences *as cultural treasures* rather than evils to be suppressed by a dominant white male minority in pursuit of its own totalitarian power.

Democracy only functions to the extent communication and debate across lines of difference is valued as the strength of a diversity that makes the struggle for mutual understanding worthwhile, because everyone understands that the treasure of achieving mutual understanding enriches ALL. When that common understanding and commitment collapses amidst the cacophony of mutually armed groups at rhetorical war with each other, all politics is reduced to a zero-sum game of struggle for the power to subdue the other, which then *normalizes the politics of violence that inevitably results in actual violence.*

The "Replacement Theory" of white nationalists is just one example of this kind of *us vs. them* non-thinking. Our resistance strategy rejects all such *us vs. them* thinking that normalizes processes of dehumanization of the other that can culminate – as history has repeatedly demonstrated in all its horror – in genocidal attempts to exterminate the other. Any individual, and any country that says this cannot happen here has not yet learned the horrible lessons that history has tried to teach us: ***It can happen here!***

What, in summary, is the proper form of political resistance/action to the propaganda of the *Big Lie*? What, at bottom, do we need to do to counter the politics of the Big Lie? We each need to start thinking – in action – and to *demand* that others stop to *think for themselves* instead of following the dictates of political propagandists and corrupt fools. And to anyone who simply throws back the junk they last heard on *Fox News* or read on their *Facebook/Meta* feed, our response is: "Stop parroting propaganda and lies, and show us you can think for yourself!" ***We must begin to demand, strengthen, and insist on the politics of truth-telling in all we do.***

Institutional Strategies for *Crushing* the Fascist Beast

Strategy #5: *Use RICO and other statutes traditionally employed against organized crime syndicates to cut off the funding sources of fascist networks, including their propaganda arms.* The project of renewing our democratic institutions of truth-telling is intimately intertwined with the project of countering the propaganda of lies dedicated to destroying these institutions. After reviewing the elements of an effective strategy for countering fascism's politics of lies, we also need to engage strategies that attack the *institutional sources* of this propaganda, *by targeting and undermining its funding sources and networks through the use of laws and prosecution methods that have always been used to take down criminal networks dedicated to the destruction of the rule of law.*

Work to strengthen our democratic institutions of truth-telling will be intimately integrated with the work needed to attack and take down the criminal sources of fascist violence on which the growth of the fascist movement depends. *Taking the offensive* against the core elements of fascist propaganda and movement building must involve a **direct attack on the movement's funding sources** in same ways we attack and cut off the funding sources of other terrorist groups. ***A fascist movement dedicated to the overthrow of our constitutional order is a terrorist movement, and it's time our institutions of law and order begin to treat* Trumpism *as the terrorist movement it is.***

Strategy #6: For the renewal and strengthening of our *democratic media*, we should establish a clear legal framework that *requires* any organization that wishes to be classified as a *news media* organization to follow basic rules of factual evidence and truth-checking in order to hold that title. Media orgs that exhibit a pattern of violating the rules of factual evidence should lose the privilege of being able to call themselves a *news* organization. And in a democracy *all media companies should be held legally accountable* for patterns of communication that attack or undermine the constitutional foundations of the nation.

Strategy #7: For the renewal and strengthening of our *judicial institutions*, the processes of judicial appointment should be de-politicized throughout the country, especially at the federal level. To begin, the Senate should outlaw the use of ideologically partisan tests or grading systems, such as those of the Federalist Society, for choosing or reviewing federal judiciary nominees. Any evidence during Senate hearings that a judicial nominee has been selected based on such ideologically partisan standards should immediately nullify the nomination for further consideration by the Senate. Lack of clear legal rules directed at protecting the independence of the judiciary from political partisanship are destroying our judiciary as a truth-telling institution, including the Supreme Court itself, as recent cases concerning abortion and voting rights have made clear.

Strategy #8: Finally, the project of democratic institution-building involves the work of renewing not only our core institutions of democracy, such as education, the judiciary, and the media, but also involves the renovation and strengthening of the core institutions of our *constitutional government.* While this essay is not intended to detail all the dimensions of this institutional work, here are some key examples.

For the renewal and strengthening of our democratic institutions of government, we should be organizing to fight for fundamental *legislative reforms* that establish clearly required (not optional) institutional guidelines for maintaining ethical integrity while serving in any elected or appointed government office:

1) There should be clear legal requirements (not just norms) for the election, appointment, or maintenance of a person in government office starting with, most logically: No person who has advocated or been involved in organizing actions to overthrow the constitutional procedures or government of the United States can be eligible for, or continue to serve in, any federal government office. Any documented evidence of planning or participation in an insurrection to overthrow the constitution or constitutional procedures of the U.S. government should ***immediately disqualify a person from election to, or continuance in government office,*** without requiring any vote by Congress. Congress should not be in charge of policing its own membership when laws are being violated. ***Clear evidence that any member of Congress has violated their oath of office to protect and defend the Constitution should earn them an immediate disqualification and ejection from office, end of story.***

2) For service in the highest political office in the country, the highest standards expected of a nominee to,

or elected holder of the presidential office should be written into law, beginning with the expectation that every nominee for president, in order to be placed on the presidential ballot, must have submitted the last ten years of their tax returns for public review. The nominee must also undergo an FBI check for prior criminal history. Any prior criminal history must be disclosed to the public, and any felonies should make a candidate ineligible to run for presidential office. Failure to disclose tax returns should immediately nullify a candidate's eligibility for presidential office. And Congress should overrule and declare null and void the DOJ ruling that places a sitting president *above the law* by making the president ineligible for felony prosecution while serving in office. Any successful felony prosecution of a President should require immediate suspension from active duty in office, with *automatic activation* of the 25th Amendment.

3) To strengthen Congressional authority as a coequal branch of government to fulfill its constitutional oversight duties, the subpoena powers of both the House and the Senate ought to be strengthened to authorize and

require Congress to utilize its *inherent contempt* powers to *swiftly arrest* anyone who defies a Congressional subpoena. Also, any Congressional referrals to the DOJ for prosecution should require the DOJ to perform an *expedited review and decision process.* Finally, any judicial overview of congressionally-ordered subpoenas of people or evidentiary materials should be required to receive *immediate and expedited judicial review.* This applies especially to any defiance of subpoenas relating to obstruction of Congress or obstruction of justice charges brought by Congress against members of the Executive branch, including the President, or against members of the House or Senate.

3. Defending Democracy:
The Political Strategy of an Effective Resistance Movement

Strategy #9: ***Protect and strengthen Voting Rights and Election administration!*** As *Part One* of this book established, the fascist movement of *Trumpism* has already entered the stage of seizing governmental power. The abundant evidence for this is clear to anyone paying attention to all the ways the Fascist GOP has been working since the January insurrection to gerrymander electoral districts, change voting laws to suppress the vote of citizens more likely to vote Democratic, and violently intimidate into retirement any local election officials dedicated to defending the integrity of our elections, in order to take control of local electoral boards. These facts make clear that ***the most urgent part of our political strategy in 2024 must be directed at halting this undemocratic seizure of power by a fascist GOP by continuing to work to defend local election boards as we continue to press Congress for the passage of strong and vibrant Voting Rights legislation.***

Our primary strategic goal must therefore be to put an end to the tactics being used by the GOP to seize government power. But then we must also initiate work toward attacking and dismantling the institutional mechanisms of recruitment that are fueling the Trumpist movement's continuing development. In other words, we must implement a strategy that simultaneously *attacks both the processes of movement recruitment and its seizure of power.* ***THIS is how we STOP the ongoing totalitarian processes of fascist development.*** The 3-

pronged framework outlined above, focused on the work of strengthening our institutions of democratic truth-telling, is the structure that will allow us to accomplish these objectives.

*****

An *effective strategy of resistance* capable of crushing the fascist beast of Trumpism will therefore require us to work together to integrate the nine specific strategies outlined above into a *structured political movement* with the following core objectives:

1) **Establish the Foundation**: Develop a new democratic political movement to defend and strengthen our core institutions of democratic citizenship: education, the news media, and our system of justice (courts, judicial appointments, systems of judicial nomination and election).

2) **Take the Offensive** against the core elements of fascist movement-building (its processes of development), including its central propaganda outlets and funding sources, which feed the fascist beast – "The best defense is an aggressive offense":

Attack and cut off the propaganda outlets and corrupt funding sources that are the primary sources of fuel sustaining and growing the Trumpist movement.

3) **Defend Democracy**. Finally, in addition to establishing the foundation of an effective resistance movement, and taking the offensive against the primary sources of support for the fascist movement, we must immediately coordinate work to:

a) STOP the ongoing work of the fascist beast to overthrow our electoral system and constitutional checks and balances for limiting the powers of the presidency.

b) STOP the fascist brownshirt tactics of violent threat, intimidation, and action by demanding that our justice systems aggressively pursue, arrest, and hold the perpetrators and leadership behind these violent tactics accountable for their crimes.

*****

History is the subject of a structure whose site is not homogeneous, empty time, but time filled with the presence of the now... [The citizen] takes cognizance of [this structure] in order to blast a specific era out of the homogeneous course of history... Thus he establishes a conception of the present as 'the time of the now' which is shot through with chips of Messianic time... For every second of time [is] the strait gate through which the Messiah might enter... In every era the attempt must be made anew to wrest tradition away from a conformism that is about to overpower it. [For] *the Messiah comes not only as the redeemer, he comes as the subduer of Antichrist.*

(Walter Benjamin, *Theses on the Philosophy of History*, XIV, XVII, XVIII, VI)

REFERENCES

Arendt, Hannah. *The Origins of Totalitarianism* [1951] (Harcourt, 1994).

Arendt, Hannah. *Eichmann in Jerusalem: A Report on the Banality of Evil* [1963] (Penguin Books, 1977).

Arendt, Hannah. *Between Past and Future: Eight Exercises in Political Thought* [1968] (Penguin Books, 1977).

Arendt, Hannah. *On Revolution* [1965] (Penguin Books, 1977).

Baldwin, James. *The Fire Next Time* (1963).

Benjamin, Walter. "Theses on the Philosophy of History," in *Illuminations: Essays and Reflections* (Schocken Books, 1968).

Fromm, Erich. *Escape from Freedom* (1941).

Frye, Northrop. *Fearful Symmetry: A Study of William Blake* (Princeton Univ. Press, 1947).

Hutchinson, Cassidy. *Enough* (Simon and Schuster, 2023).

Jaspers, Karl. *The Future of Mankind* [1958], trans. by E. B. Ashton (University of Chicago Press, 1961).

Jaspers, Karl. *Philosophy and the World: Selected Essays* [1958], trans. by E. B. Ashton (Regnery Gateway, 1963).

Kierkegaard, Soren. *For Self-Examination and Judge for Yourselves!* [1851], trans. by Walter Lowrie (Princeton Univ. Press, 1941).

King, David. *The Trial of Adolf Hitler: The Beer Hall Putsch and the Rise of Nazi Germany* (W.W. Norton, 2017).

Kraus, Karl. *The Last Days of Mankind* [1922], trans. by Fred Bridgham and Edward Timms (Yale Univ. Press, 2015).

Kraus, Karl. *The Third Walpurgis Night* [1933], trans. by Fred Bridgham and Edward Timms (Yale Univ. Press, 2020).

Levinas, Emmanuel. "Truth of Disclosure and Truth of Testimony," 1972 (In *Emmanuel Levinas: Basic Philosophical Writings*, 1996).

Machiavelli, Niccolo. *The Discourses* (Penguin Books, 1998).

Paxton, Robert O. *The Anatomy of Fascism* (Vintage Books, 2004).

Rothkopf, David. *Traitor: A History of American Betrayal from Benedict Arnold to Donald Trump* (Thomas Dunne Books, 2020).

Snyder, Timothy. *On Tyranny: Twenty Lessons from the Twentieth Century* (Tim Duggan Books, 2017).

Stanley, Jason. *How Fascism Works: The Politics of Us and Them* (Random House, 2018).

The Trump Indictments: The 91 Criminal Counts Against the Former President of the United States, edited and introduced by Ali Velshi (Mariner Books [HarperCollins], 2023).

Weissmann, Andrew. Where Law Ends: Inside the Mueller Investigation (Random House, 2020).

9 798224 751754